A RETREAT WITH BENEDICT AND BERNARD

Other titles in the
A Retreat With... *Series:*

A RETREAT WITH
BENEDICT AND BERNARD

Seeking God Alone—Together

Linus Mundy

ST. ANTHONY MESSENGER PRESS

Cincinnati, Ohio

Excerpts from *No Moment Too Small: Rhythms of Silence, Prayer and Holy Reading,* by Norvene Vest, copyright ©1994, *The Cistercian Way,* by Andre Louf, copyright ©1983, *Bernard of Clairvaux and the Cistercian Spirit,* by Jean Leclerq, O.S.B., copyright ©1976, and *The Difficult Saint: Bernard of Clairvaux and His Tradition,* by Brian P. McGuire, copyright ©1991, are used by permission of Cistercian Publications.

The excerpt from *Always We Begin Again: The Benedictine Way of Living,* copyright ©1996 John McQuiston II, is reprinted by permission of Morehouse Publishing.

The excerpt from "Bernard of Clairvaux as a Spiritual Director," *Cistercian Studies Quarterly,* Vol. XXIII (1988) is used by permission.

Excerpts from *Meditations: On the Monk Who Dwells in Daily Life,* by Thomas Moore, copyright ©1995, and "Living With Contradiction: Reflections on the Rule of St. Benedict," by Esther De Waal, from *A Life-Giving Way: A Commentary on the Rule of St. Benedict,* copyright ©1989, are used by permission of HarperCollins.

The excerpt from *PAX: The Benedictine Way,* by Ambrose Tinsley, O.S.B., is used by permission of The Columba Press Limited.

Cover illustrations by Steve Erspamer, S.M.
Cover and book design by Mary Alfieri
Electronic format and pagination by Sandy L. Digman

ISBN 0-86716-301-1

*T*O *D*AVE *S*TIPP,
   the most everyday monk
   I've ever known

Contents

Introducing A Retreat With...

Twenty years ago I made a weekend retreat at a Franciscan house on the coast of New Hampshire. The retreat director's opening talk was as lively as a long-range weather forecast. He told us how completely God loves each one of us—without benefit of lively anecdotes or fresh insights.

As the friar rambled on, my inner critic kept up a sotto voce commentary: "I've heard all this before." "Wish he'd say something new that I could chew on." "That poor man really doesn't have much to say." Ever hungry for manna yet untasted, I devalued any experience of hearing the same old thing.

After a good night's sleep, I awoke feeling as peaceful as a traveler who has at last arrived safely home. I walked across the room toward the closet. On the way I passed the sink with its small framed mirror on the wall above. Something caught my eye like an unexpected presence. I turned, saw the reflection in the mirror and said aloud, "No wonder he loves me!"

This involuntary affirmation stunned me. What or whom had I seen in the mirror? When I looked again, it was "just me," an ordinary person with a lower-than-average reservoir of self-esteem. But I knew that in the initial vision I had seen God-in-me breaking through like a sudden sunrise.

At that moment I knew what it meant to be made in the divine image. I understood right down to my size eleven feet what it meant to be loved exactly as I was. Only later did I connect this revelation with one granted to the Trappist monk-writer Thomas Merton. As he reports in *Conjectures of a Guilty Bystander*, while standing all unsuspecting on a street corner one day, he was overwhelmed by the "joy of being...a member of a race in which God Himself became incarnate.... There is no way of telling people that they are all walking around shining like the sun."

As an absentminded homemaker may leave a wedding ring on the kitchen windowsill, so I have often mislaid this precious conviction. But I have never forgotten that particular retreat. It persuaded me that the Spirit rushes in where it will. Not even a boring director or a judgmental retreatant can withstand the "violent wind" that "fills the entire house" where we dwell in expectation (see Acts 2:2).

So why deny ourselves any opportunity to come aside awhile and rest on holy ground? Why not withdraw from the daily web that keeps us muddled and wound? Wordsworth's complaint is ours as well: "The world is too much with us." There is no flu shot to protect us from infection by the skepticism of the media, the greed of commerce, the alienating influence of technology. We need retreats as the deer needs the running stream.

An Invitation

This book and its companions in the *A Retreat With...* series from St. Anthony Messenger Press are designed to meet that need. They are an invitation to choose as director some of the most powerful, appealing and wise mentors our faith tradition has to offer.

Our directors come from many countries, historical

eras and schools of spirituality. At times they are teamed to sing in close harmony (for example, Francis de Sales, Jane de Chantal and Aelred of Rievaulx on spiritual friendship). Others are paired to kindle an illuminating fire from the friction of their differing views (such as Augustine of Hippo and Mary Magdalene on human sexuality). All have been chosen because, in their humanness and their holiness, they can help us grow in self-knowledge, discernment of God's will and maturity in the Spirit.

Inviting us into relationship with these saints and holy ones are inspired authors from today's world, women and men whose creative gifts open our windows to the Spirit's flow. As a motto for the authors of our series, we have borrowed the advice of Dom Frederick Dunne to the young Thomas Merton. Upon joining the Trappist monks, Merton wanted to sacrifice his writing activities lest they interfere with his contemplative vocation. Dom Frederick wisely advised, "Keep on writing books that make people love the spiritual life."

That is our motto. Our purpose is to foster (or strengthen) friendships between readers and retreat directors—friendships that feed the soul with wisdom, past and present. Like the scribe "trained for the kingdom of heaven," each author brings forth from his or her storeroom "what is new and what is old" (Matthew 13:52).

The Format

The pattern for each *A Retreat With...* remains the same; readers of one will be in familiar territory when they move on to the next. Each book is organized as a seven-session retreat that readers may adapt to their own schedules or to the needs of a group.

Day One begins with an anecdotal introduction called "Getting to Know Our Directors." Readers are given a telling glimpse of the guides with whom they will be sharing the retreat experience. A second section, "Placing Our Directors in Context," will enable retreatants to see the guides in their own historical, geographical, cultural and spiritual settings.

Having made the human link between seeker and guide, the authors go on to "Introducing Our Retreat Theme." This section clarifies how the guide(s) are especially suited to explore the theme and how the retreatant's spirituality can be nourished by it.

After an original "Opening Prayer" to breathe life into the day's reflection, the author, speaking with and through the mentor(s), will begin to spin out the theme. While focusing on the guide(s)' own words and experience, the author may also draw on Scripture, tradition, literature, art, music, psychology or contemporary events to illuminate the path.

Each day's session is followed by reflection questions designed to challenge, affirm and guide the reader in integrating the theme into daily life. A "Closing Prayer" brings the session full circle and provides a spark of inspiration for the reader to harbor until the next session.

Days Two through Six begin with "Coming Together in the Spirit" and follow a format similar to Day One. Day Seven weaves the entire retreat together, encourages a continuation of the mentoring relationship and concludes with "Deepening Your Acquaintance," an envoi to live the theme by God's grace, the director(s)' guidance and the retreatant's discernment. A closing section of Resources serves as a larder from which readers may draw enriching books, videos, cassettes and films.

We hope readers will experience at least one of those memorable "No wonder God loves me!" moments. And we hope that they will have "talked back" to the mentors, as good friends are wont to do.

A case in point: There was once a famous preacher who always drew a capacity crowd to the cathedral. Whenever he spoke, an eccentric old woman sat in the front pew directly beneath the pulpit. She took every opportunity to mumble complaints and contradictions— just loud enough for the preacher to catch the drift that he was not as wonderful as he was reputed to be. Others seated down front glowered at the woman and tried to shush her. But she went right on needling the preacher to her heart's content.

When the old woman died, the congregation was astounded at the depth and sincerity of the preacher's grief. Asked why he was so bereft, he responded, "Now who will help me to grow?"

All of our mentors in *A Retreat With...* are worthy guides. Yet none would seek retreatants who simply said, "Where you lead, I will follow. You're the expert." In truth, our directors provide only half the retreat's content. Readers themselves will generate the other half.

As general editor for the retreat series, I pray that readers will, by their questions, comments, doubts and decision-making, fertilize the seeds our mentors have planted.

And may the Spirit of God rush in to give the growth.

Gloria Hutchinson
Series Editor
Conversion of Saint Paul

Getting to Know Our Directors

You are reading this book because you know there is a "monk soul" deep inside of you.

There's one inside of me, too.

More "officially," there are approximately 9,000 "real" Benedictine monks, 8,000 Benedictine nuns and 11,500 Benedictine sisters in our world. As to the Cistercians (the order in which Saint Bernard was an early abbot), there are now approximately 3,000 Cistercian monks and 4,000 nuns.

But just what is a monk? Some wise Benedictine once suggested that he is one who asks every day—"What is a monk?"

And then there's us. Monks and nuns don't have a monopoly on loving God, on holiness, on striving for goodness. We, too, are to ask ourselves something each day—"What is a Christian?"

This book is intended to be a motivator to help us ask that question—and begin to answer it in ways that are both universal and unique, not unlike the two mentors of this retreat experience.

I first came to know Benedict at home—and Bernard away from home. It was my parents whose schoolteachers throughout their formative childhood years were Benedictine sisters and whose parish priests were Benedictine monks. The same experiences were to be mine. The lived Benedictine values of work and prayer were all around and within us as children: Indeed, was there anything else to life besides work and prayer? If so, it was kept from us country folks, except on those wonderful, rare occasions when our cousins came in from the city to play in our "desert"! (Our city cousins, in actuality, were small-town cousins to our farm family. But even so, they had things like orange juice for breakfast; they drove up in shinier cars; they played more sophisticated games than we did. To further distinguish themselves from us, they wore shoes when they went out to play—even in the summertime!) Maybe this is a big part of the reason I can relate to the simplicity and austerity of the monastic life.

At age thirteen, I became even more deeply steeped in the life and traditions of Holy Benedict. I chose to attend Saint Meinrad, a Benedictine seminary in Indiana, run by a community of more than one hundred and fifty monks. At Saint Meinrad, it wasn't work and prayer; it was *ora et labora*. The stakes had been raised; Benedict's sacred motto—like so much else back then—was decreed to us in Latin. And Latin—like monasticism and like God—was mysterious and special. Anyone can easily recite "Prefer nothing to the work of the Lord." But when it is rendered, as Benedict rendered it, *"Operi Dei nihil praeponatur,"* it takes on a whole new level of mystery—and sacredness.

I also learned at Saint Meinrad that it does, in fact, take a village to raise a child.

Not until I was in my thirties did I choose to raise the stakes higher for myself. I began to explore the hidden and mysterious Trappist monks of Kentucky. To me, at the time, this was the ultimate in both mystery and sacredness. From what I had heard of the Trappists, these were people who reduced everything to its bare essence.

I had always remembered as a boy there being a holy man in our little town. His name, oddly enough, was Bernard. He was not like the rest of the men in town (except for maybe my Dad, who was also a very gentle and holy soul). Bernard had a smile and a style that everyone loved. His eyes sparkled. It would not be fair to describe him as different, but he was special. Contemplative. One day Bernard simply disappeared, and the word was only that he had gone off to join a monastery somewhere. Later I found out he joined the Trappists of Kentucky. Indeed, his body is now buried not far from the grave of another Trappist monk, Thomas Merton. I was deeply moved when I first happened upon Bernard's grave there.

But it was partly this holy man, Bernard, from my little town, that drew me to Saint Bernard and the Trappists (or as they are more officially known, monks of the Order of Cistercians of the Strict Observance). Notice, I said I began to explore the Trappists, not *become* a Trappist. Happily married and a proud father, I could only join them figuratively (which, I am reminded, is somewhat akin to becoming a vegetarian between meals!).

The very first time I went to visit the Trappists at Gethsemani in Kentucky, I was running just a bit late for my first dinner there. I got to the dining room and filed past the food line with my tray, disappointed that they were out of the main dish; all that was left was a big pan of whole, boiled onions. When I took my seat with the rest of the retreatants, I found that the boiled onion *was* the main dish!

So why do so many thousands today make Benedictinism and Cistercianism their main dish? Why do so many hundreds of thousands of people on the sidelines fall in love with the lives and ways of Benedictines and Cistercians/Trappists? One simple answer is: Because they're there. But there are many other answers.

Someday I want to tell more of my own love story about them and my debt to them. As a matter of fact, I want to write a novel about my experiences and call it something like "The Dead Monks' Society." It would be about this middle-aged married guy with three children (that's me) who pays nightly visits to a monastery graveyard. And what does he do at the graveyard? He seeks advice from the society of dead monks there, of course! He seeks advice about real-world issues like raising a family, trying to be a good husband, the meaning of work, finances, gardening, mid-life, taking care of oneself, the death of a parent, being a good dad. One clear difference in this novel from so many others is that I couldn't have one of those disclaimers up front in the book that says: "This is a work of fiction; any resemblances to persons living or dead," etc. This novel would be about living and dead people who have given their gifts to me. And who keep on giving.

At Saint Meinrad Archabbey's monastery graveyard, I have counted nearly two dozen gravesites worth paying a visit for real-world advice—monks I've known personally over the years who during their lives taught me so much. At the cemetery on the grounds of the Trappist Abbey of Gethsemani, there are more monks to pray with and to for help (including the grave, of course, of Thomas Merton, whom I've come to know through his writings and talks).

I spent five years in a Benedictine seminary and have been associated in one way or another with them since then. I have also been going to the Abbey of Gethsemani for retreat a few times a year for nearly twenty years now. What continues to seem so natural to me—and yet at the same time so astounding—is the incredible relevance of "that thing that monks do" to people like you and me!

While our retreat directors Benedict of Nursia and Bernard of Clairvaux never knew each other personally (there was half a millennium between them), they were remarkably alike in that they were of one mind: *God's mind*.

For this very reason, in Benedict and Bernard, I think

we have the ideal teacher-directors for our week-long spiritual time together as God-seekers. What better way to go deeper into the present than to go deep into the past for spiritual grounding—to two sources who lived the questions we live, who faced the very questions that are so inescapable for any modern seeker: Who is God in my life? Where am I going with my life? Is there a better way? What is a monk? What is a Christian?

What especially bonds both Benedict and Bernard for me is the intensity of their message. They both challenge us seekers to reduce the God-and-us relationship to its essence, just as Christ's gospel dictates: by way of love, pure and simple.

Introducing Benedict of Nursia

Heralded as the founder of all Western monasticism, Benedict was born in C.E. 480 in Nursia, Italy. His family was of comfortable means. He went to Rome as a student, and there reacted to the open godlessness of his peers and the general corruption of his society by retreating to an underground cave in the hills of Subiaco. He lived there as a self-declared hermit for three years, working out his personal conversion of mind and heart to God.

In a short time, his reputation as a holy person spread, and disciples came to him, pleading with him to found a monastery. Some cynics might say these followers were like spiritual fortune hunters, hoping to ride along on the coattails of an insider. Nonetheless, they recognized Benedict as a holy person with a plan. The same could no doubt be said of Saints Francis and Clare of Assisi, Ignatius of Loyola and Teresa of Avila, and of Thomas Merton, Gandhi, Mother Teresa, Dorothy Day—and Jesus. Many recognized them as special bearers of divine light—

perhaps even miracle workers—and thus flocked to them as followers, whether these leaders wanted such followers or not.

With Benedict, his followers formed a religious order of monks dedicated first and foremost to conversion, to a turning to God's ways, "to prefer nothing to Christ," *Ut in omnia glorificetur Deo...* ("That in all things God may be glorified"). It was the linchpin of an entire code or "rule" that Benedict created. In the retreat days that follow, we will delve into many of the particulars of Benedict's Rule or system and work to apply them to our own lives.

Benedict then made his way to Monte Cassino, where he transformed the ruined Roman temples of Jupiter and Apollo into what was to become the greatest monastery in Christendom. Benedict's sister, Scholastica, lived near Monte Cassino as head of a nunnery. Benedict died at Monte Cassino on March 21, 547. During his lifetime, Benedict's Holy Rule, now familiarly known as the Holy Rule of Saint Benedict, was used as the guide for the monks of twelve separate monasteries that he headed for eighteen years.

What is this Holy Rule all about? Ultimately, Benedict agreed with the early Church which believed that monastic life could best foster one's spiritual development. By way of the discipline and graces of this special blend of liturgical and community life, individuals achieved advancement of the soul in a monastery as they could nowhere else. That was the belief then, and it still is the belief of many today.

But just what was it that made Benedict's principles or system of spirituality—the Rule—such a practical and foolproof one? The Rule is based on the gospel and is intended solely as a way to live the gospel. And that means that above all it emphasizes *conversion*. We'll talk much more about this all-important topic in Day One of our retreat.

Benedict intended that the life of a monk consist of manual labor, reading and the liturgy of the Church. Further, the monastery itself was to be a home—the monks make up the family, with the abbot as the father (in a women's religious order, the abbess is the mother) and the Rule as the family touchstone, providing the rhythmic daily pattern of work, study, community and prayer.

Historically speaking, it was thanks to Benedict's Rule that something quite amazing took place: In effect, the Rule of Saint Benedict revitalized the entire monastic movement in Europe. Benedictine monks not only established monasteries throughout the continent, but their monasteries, cathedrals and universities were also the leading institutions that remained after the collapse of the Roman Empire. Indeed, by the time of the Reformation, no fewer than fifty popes, thirty emperors and ninety-seven kings and queens were, or claimed to be, Benedictine. Monasteries of men, and women, were widespread—and vibrant.

Regrettably, as time went on, things eroded. As the Benedictine movement became a secular and political power, it departed from its origins and values, and its influence declined for many centuries. And then—compressing a lot of time into a sentence—Bernard was among those who revitalized the Benedictine movement. And now, readers of such books as this are the revitalizers of today, recognizing that Benedict and his Rule remain time-tested guides to a most profound life of the spirit.

A final word here about Benedict and the Rule: Benedict was a layman; he was never a priest. And his Rule was written for the laity. All monasticism was essentially, at its origins, a lay movement. Agreed, monasticism in time became much more clerical—that is, in monasteries of men, more and more of the members came to be ordained to the priesthood. Yet its deepest roots are in a common ground—ground that we, too, walk on, whether women or men, lay or ordained, monk or ordinary Christian.

Introducing Bernard of Clairvaux

Bernard of Clairvaux, though he lived some six hundred years after Benedict, is somewhat more mysterious to us than Benedict. And perhaps even more interesting! Some would say there are "two" Bernards: one, the abbot locked away in the silence of the cloister; the other, a strident ecclesiastical politician, pushing and pulling everyone into the monastery and its life-style. (Indeed, he ended up bringing every member of his family into the monastery—and, in that sense, he was different from most monks, both contemporary and later, who are required to break away from friends and family to become a monk in a contemplative community.)

Bernard was born in 1090, of Burgundian nobility. (To me, that means he was French—and pretty well off.) Early in life, he showed promise as a poet. Indeed, he was said to have penned the insight: "We can learn more from the woods, from stones and trees, than from teachers and books." (A hint here of his future as a great mystical writer?) At the death of his mother, Bernard's life was transformed, and he joined the austere Cistercians, an order of primitive Benedictine monks. It has been said of Bernard by tongue-in-cheek commentators: "Afflicted with anemia, migraine, gastritis, hypertension, and an atrophied sense of taste, Bernard had obvious monastic leadership potential; he soon founded his own monastery."[1]

Thus it was that in 1113 Bernard arrived—with some thirty relatives and friends—at the religious monastic community at Citeaux in France. Bernard's abbot there was Stephen Harding, one of the better-known adherents to a stricter interpretation of the Holy Rule of Saint Benedict than was in vogue at the time. Bernard, seeking nothing less than spiritual perfection, was the perfect apostle. In fact, it was Bernard who was sent out by Stephen Harding in 1115 to found a new Cistercian monastery at Clairvaux.

Found it he did—and a lot of other wonderful things. Bernard went on to become a powerful evangelist for the Cistercian Order. Some go so far as to say the entire Order would no longer exist if not for Bernard's vitality. (Note: While he is often mistaken as the founder of the Cistercians, he wasn't. Robert, abbot of the Benedictine Abbey of Molesme, and twenty-one followers founded the Abbey of Citeaux in 1098. Here, they observed Benedict's Rule in all its strictness. However, following Bernard's lifetime, the Cistercians from Citeaux were often called "Bernardines.") Indeed, Bernard would climb practically any mountain and cross any sea to sing of the virtues of this style of monastic life. His contention was simply that monastic life provided the very best means of attaining holiness. Period. One amusing legend has it that Bernard went so far as to convince the Count of Champagne to cut down a thief about to be hanged and have him turned over to Clairvaux in order to secure for the man a far harsher punishment—as a monk![2]

Why study Bernard and the witness of the Cistercians? Again: Because they're there. And that alone is a pretty remarkable reason. They have survived the test of time. But better: Because they boiled down the life of the Christ-follower to its essence. Though some scholars would take the following as a bit too simplistic, the Cistercians were true "reductionists." It was the Cistercians—this branch of the Benedictines—who reduced the spiritual quest to two words: God alone.

Some historians say this was the singular goal of

Bernard and of the earliest reformers of Benedictinism, the Cistercians: They saw themselves as keepers of the vision. In their eyes, with their vision, these reformers ("re-discoverers"?) saw the good work and ways of Benedict being degenerated by the saint's followers over the five hundred to six hundred years since his death. It was all getting too easy to be a monk now, and so they sought to bring back Benedict's authentic, original mission and vision to their Order. And then they added their own interpretations. Among other purposes, they sought to raise the stakes.

This they did with full abandon, as we shall see later in this work, and as any visit to a modern-day Trappist monastery may still attest. (The Trappists I speak of are those of the O.C.S.O.: the Order of Cistercians of the Strict Observance. Their official name tells us a lot! There are also Cistercians of the Common Observance.) In Bernard's own time, scholar Jean Leclercq, O.S.B., tells us that the Cistercians, "in Bernard's charismatic shadow, grew from two small, poor monasteries to over 300...." At Clairvaux alone, Bernard headed seven hundred monks. "Refusing class privilege, they balanced manual labor and liturgical prayer with private reading and solitary meditation. Critical of affluent and comfortable monks, Cistercians ruthlessly discarded everything which might distract them from their goal: the experiential knowledge of God."[3]

Bernard's route to holiness for himself and his followers was a hard one. But it's also important to recognize Bernard's compassion. Yes, there is clear evidence that Bernard sided with a stricter observance of the Benedictine Holy Rule—he was accused by some of being quite fanatical, compulsively locked into his own regime of asceticism. And some have written that Bernard demanded more of his brothers than ordinary humans could ever give! But Bernard could also be a merciful parent to his monastic family. Witness the following story:

> There is...the story of how one day, when he was
> preaching to the monks in chapter, he realized that
> most of them were looking quite downcast and
> discouraged. He then gave them what is called a
> *magnificum verbum*, a wonderful saying, promising
> that if his monks remained in the Cistercian Order
> and died in its habit, they would all be saved. Even
> Judas, he assured them, if he had become a
> Cistercian, would have been able to gain salvation!
> Bernard...preached penance and asceticism, but he
> knew he was dealing with people who could get
> depressed and feel everything was too difficult.[4]

So it was that Bernard, unlike Benedict, did not create or
possess a "new" Holy Rule to live by; rather, he refused to
accept the status quo; he argued vehemently and tirelessly
for something "more perfect" and more in harmony with
what he saw as God's plan and will. Concludes biographer
Brian P. McGuire: "Bernard will have to remain for us...a
mysterious combination of affection and hostility, a tireless
ally, an unpredictable opponent.... As with Anselm,
Francis of Assisi, or Jesus himself, Bernard remains an
enigma, an object of love and a focus of hostility."[5]

One sure sign of the respect of his own contemporaries
within the Church is the fact that Bernard was canonized a
saint in 1174, just twenty-one years after his death. In 1830,
he was formally recognized as a doctor (major teacher) of
the Church.

And what is Bernard's unique legacy? The first is the
intense enthusiasm this fiery founder of many monasteries
shows us. Indeed, he was one incredible, paradoxical
blend of vigorous action and mystical contemplation. (The
bi-polar in all of us can relate to that.)

But the other major contribution of Bernard is this: He
left a legacy of monastic friendship. It is his absolutely

unique contribution to us. Others may argue that it was Bernard's holiness, his intellect, or his writings which exerted so profound an influence on Roman Catholic spirituality. But despite the fact that Christ told us again and again in the Gospels of the need to leave mother and father, brother and sister, Bernard demonstrated a way of conversion that brought family and friends along on this new and more direct path to holiness. For Bernard, the process of conversion was a family affair:

> William of Thierry's account [Bernard's first biographer] of Bernard's conversion to the monastic life describes this process in such a natural and inevitable manner that one can fail to notice how original Bernard was on insisting on entering Citeaux not alone but in the company of family members and good friends. If we look...we can see that Bernard's decision to enter Citeaux did not take place from one day to the next. First he decided on the monastic life. Then he went about convincing his brothers and near relations and friends to accompany him. The whole band settled down for a while on the family property and made themselves ready for the great move. Only then did Bernard and his brothers and friends come knocking on the door of Citeaux. Abbot Stephen was not confronted with a few individuals who had gotten together by chance in the last stages of their decision to become monks. He had to deal with a well-coordinated and determined group of people who had prepared themselves not just to enter a monastery but also to maintain their bonds to each other and yet to alter them radically within the context of monastic life. Stephen took on friends who intended to continue being each other's friends in more exciting ways than they ever could experience in the world of the school or of the castle.[6]

It is stated in the Cistercian constitutions and statutes:

> Cistercian monks seek God and follow Christ under
> a rule and an abbot in a stable community that is a
> school of brotherly love. Since all the brothers are of
> one heart and one mind, they have everything in
> common. By bearing one another's burdens they
> fulfill Christ's law, participating in his sufferings in
> the hope of entering the kingdom of heaven.[7]

Most fascinating to me is that some scholars have argued
that one of Bernard's most celebrated treatises, *On the Love
of God*, contains teachings that could just as well be lived
out in a marriage as in a monastery. (Yes!)

How tough was it at Clairvaux in Bernard's time?
Bernard himself penned the following poetic words:

> A driver of oxen must have two things: a sweet
> voice, to soften the labour of those who toil; the prick
> of a goad, to rouse the torpor of those who flag.[8]

What follows is a sort of "Point-Counterpoint" answer
you may also enjoy as much as I have. Both of these
quotes are from letters between Bernard and Aelred of
Rievaulx, a fellow Cistercian and also a spiritual master.
Here is Bernard's own description of Clairvaux:

> Yes, if you would know, it is Clairvaux. She is
> Jerusalem, joined to that which is heaven.... Do not
> the mountains [here] drip with sweetness, and the
> hills flow with milk and honey...?[9]

And here—the "counterpoint"— from Abbot Aelred,
speaking in the person of a novice:

> Our food is scanty, our garments rough; our drink is
> from the stream and our sleep often upon our book.
> Under our limbs there is but a hard mat; when sleep
> is sweetest we must rise at a bell's bidding.[10]

Finally, we would also do well to remember something

else. My friend, Eugene Hensell, O.S.B., himself a wise student of both Benedict and Bernard, reminds me that in both Benedict's and Bernard's times, the monastery was somewhat of a haven—especially compared to the peasant life that most folks were experiencing. Further, folks didn't live as long back then as we do today. They knew, therefore—much better than we who keep working feverishly at prolonging life and putting off our last breath as long as we possibly can—that most of life was after death! Does that mean monastic life was easy? No. But we need not look at it as being quite as austere in the relative scheme of things as we are prone to do. In fact, the modern monk, and perhaps especially the premodern monk of only a generation or two or three ago was one who wrote the book on austerity—as relative to the world where most of us dwell.

What Bernard seemed to believe—and practice and preach—was that the monastic way was really Christ's way. Bernard believed that those who observed the Rule of Saint Benedict were actually reproducing the life-style of the apostles. Just as the apostles were invited to "Come, follow me," by Christ, monks were called to leave all behind and follow Christ by embracing a life of poverty, austerity and prayer. Wrote Bernard to his would-be followers:

> The apostles left all and gathered together in the school of the Saviour,...in hunger and thirst, in cold and nakedness, in toil and fasting. So do you, and though you are not their equals in merit, you are made to some degree their peers by your practice.[11]

Placing Our Directors in Context

Today as I write this, I have just returned from one of the largest churches in my home state. It's St. Benedict Church in Evansville, Indiana. I'm staying at a quiet "writing spot" just two blocks away from the church here in this Midwestern city. And even here, as everywhere, Benedict's legacy continues. The Mass I attended this morning was celebrated by a Benedictine monk (who also happened to be one of my Latin teachers some thirty years ago). Monte Cassino in Italy or some other great European or American Benedictine abbey this St. Benedict Church is not—but, even so, some one hundred or more faithful attended Mass this weekday morning to unite with Benedict and Christ in praising God.

Other Benedictine traditions are undeniably gaining strength in our own era and beyond this city in which I write: Today there is a mounting hunger for things monastic, for things Benedictine. Just look at the international popularity of a certain Gregorian chant album and the ten-month waiting lists at monastery retreat houses such as the one at the Abbey of Gethsemani in central Kentucky. Consider the popularity of books like *The Cloister Walk* by Kathleen Norris and *Virgin Time* by Patricia Hampl. Indeed, monks and "monkhood" are getting to be pretty respectable again!

In Benedict's and Bernard's times, there were similar hungers to those we know firsthand. Benedict readily recognized the need in his own life for "a better way" to God; he radically shaped that better way for himself and for centuries of followers with his Rule and his lived example.

Bernard, too, hungered for more—and his method of getting more was by way of less: by way of just the spiritual essentials. As a modern follower puts it: "You and me, God—and mostly you!" Or as the motto inscribed in marble starkly greets one at the entrance to the Trappist Abbey of Gethsemani: "God alone." (It is also no accident, I think, that one must pass directly through the center of a cemetery to enter the retreat house and church.)

Author Wendy Wright helps put both Benedict and Bernard into her historical context for us in a companion volume in this series, *A Retreat With Francis de Sales, Jane de Chantal and Aelred of Rievaulx: Befriending Each Other in God*:

> The Church, like any human institution—political, economic or cultural—constantly changes. Each generation must internalize the faith anew.... The Benedictine rule had governed most monasteries for centuries, but [in the twelfth century, Bernard's time] observance had been adapted to the needs of increasingly wealthy and organizationally complex monasteries that had come to function as economic and political powers in feudal Europe.
>
> Under the leadership of men like Bernard of Clairvaux, the primitive simplicity of Benedictine life was restored.... Founding their houses in secluded areas, the Cistercian monks lived austerely, alternating their time with manual labor and prayer. Their prayer was primarily (but not exclusively) communal. The community gathered at appointed times and immersed themselves in Scripture, thus creating an atmosphere of continued and deepening recollection. Those who were drawn to the Cistercians, like Aelred [and Bernard] of the twelfth century and Thomas Merton of the twentieth, were men and women who took the spiritual life with the utmost seriousness.[12]

The core of Cistercian life, Wright goes on to tell us, was a spirituality shaped by the monastic life-style, yet deeply "imbued with the humanistic optimism of that era." The Cistercians of the time considered themselves participating in Christ's life by participating in Christ's martyrdom—his ultimate sacrifice on the cross. Thus the ideal monk follows Christ's example and "dies to self," dies to greed and luxury and comfort and power and self-importance. Instead, one strips down to the essentials (to God alone) via mortification, obedience, humility, charity, purity of heart.

Just as with Benedict, Bernard's version of Cistercian life emphasized this community aspect of the transforming monastic venture. Monks in community know, as enlightened families everywhere know, that "people go home together to God" (in Wendy Wright's beautiful phrase). It is only later that the *social* gospel, social action outside the "family"—namely, out in the larger family of humanity, out in the world—takes center stage and is fully embodied within religious orders and communities such as the Franciscans, the Dominicans and the Jesuits.

Benedict and Bernard, like most of us, stayed home. (Well, mostly....)

Notes

[1] Sean Kelly and Rosemary Rogers, *Saints Preserve Us!* (New York: Random House, 1993), p. 40.

[2] Brian P. McGuire, *The Difficult Saint: Bernard of Clairvaux and His Tradition* (Kalamazoo, Mich.: Cistercian Publications, 1991), p. 27.

[3] Jean Leclercq, O.S.B., *Bernard of Clairvaux and the Cistercian Spirit* (Kalamazoo, Mich.: Cistercian Publications, 1976), back cover.

[4] McGuire.

[5] Ibid.

[6] Ibid.

[7] *Constitutions and Statutes of the Monks and Nuns of the Cistercian Order of the Strict Observance and Other Legislative Documents.*

[8] Jean Leclercq, O.S.B., *The Influence of Saint Bernard* (Oxford, England: SLG Press, 1976), p. xvi.

[9] Letter 64 of Benedict quoted in David Knowles, *Christian Monasticism* (New York: McGraw Hill, World University Library, 1969), p. 90.

[10] Aelred, *The Mirror of Friendship,* as quoted in Knowles, p. 90.

[11] C. H. Lawrence, *Medieval Monasticism: Forms of Religious Life in Western Europe in the Middle Ages* (Essex, England: Longman, 1989), p. 184.

[12] Wendy Wright, *A Retreat With Francis de Sales, Jane de Chantal and Aelred of Rievaulx: Befriending One Another in God* (Cincinnati: St. Anthony Messenger Press, 1996), pp. 16, 17.

Day One

A Vow to Always Begin Again (Conversion)

Introducing Our Retreat Theme

This retreat is all about seeking God alone—together. And that means, above all, converting, *changing*—alone and together. This was Benedict's foremost vow, and it was the singular goal of Bernard and his followers.

"Every day I say to myself—Today I will begin." This "daily vow of conversion" comes from Saint Antony of the Desert, who preceded Benedict and Bernard, but who greatly inspired both of them.

A word about vows: In this book, I refer to the word vow in every chapter title. And by that I mean only a "commitment to oneself" or "statement or declaration in one's mind." So I use the term figuratively only—or, better, I'm applying the word in its more simple root definition as a "pledge" or "promise" or "intent." Thus the reader is not encouraged to "take a vow" in the binding, traditional religious sense of the word, but rather in the sense of making a firm resolution. A vow in its most solemn sense is a binding commitment, under penalty of sin (whether slight sin or grave).

The vows that monks take—as the vows that married people take—are serious. And for monks, some of the vows are temporary; some are permanent or perpetual.

Just as it is a common belief that Benedict and all the early monks were ordained folks and not laypersons, there is also the common belief today that the always-and-forever vows taken by Benedictines (and their offshoot, the Cistercians) were poverty, chastity and obedience. Wrong! In point of fact, Benedict's first vow for himself and his followers was, simply, a vow to change. It was a vow of *conversion*—to "always begin again."

And it was a vow for ordinary folks. Benedict and Bernard both bring this home to us, in their own distinct, yet common, ways.

Trappist monk of Gethsemani Matthew Kelty likens a monastery to a support group, a family that's "in this thing together." Any visitor to a monastery can readily feel that the monastery is a place of healing rhythms, an anchor, a stake in the ground, but it is the monk who lives there who can attest to the "family system," the "household of God" that a monastic community can be when it is at its best. While solitude is much respected, Benedictines and Cistercians know that solitude must be balanced with community, for if one is alone with the self, it becomes too easy to make the self the center of life.

There is nothing like community itself—and a family is nothing but a small community—to facilitate change. I read recently about a law of physics that intrigues me. It goes something like this: "That which we observe we change." I think the key word here is *observe*. In families, we are truly observed—and often when we don't want to be! ("Mike, will you leave me alone!" "Emily, didn't I just say your father and I wanted some time alone?") But, put under observation, families and communities can together observe and identify those things that could use some conversion: "John, I bet Sara would help you if you said 'Please' once in awhile." "Honey, what say this year at

Christmas we sing carols at the nursing home instead of in our neighborhood?"

Opening Prayer

> God,
> we pray to be available to you,
> that's all.
> We want to listen
> to the beating of your drum
> as well as the whisper of your
> Spirit.
> Teach us what to do,
> where to go and how to act,
> Yes...
> But most of all
> teach us to sit still
> and know that you are our God,
> and we are your children,
> your sisters and brothers,
> your partners
> and friends,
> together.
> Amen.

RETREAT SESSION ONE
Converting to Singlemindedness

John Cardinal Newman once said that to be good, one must change, and to be perfect, one must change often.

An interesting case in point is the life of Bernard, who indeed changed often. Remember the saying that "A foolish consistency is the hobgoblin of little minds"? Bernard did not have a little mind! Among other stances, Bernard was a leading proponent of the Second Crusade, only to see himself end up on the short end of this losing, misguided proposition; he also strongly sought the condemnation of the teachings of philosopher Peter Abelard, whose views were seen as a bit too radical for Bernard; and yet it was Bernard who could be a most tender and forgiving abbot, as we note elsewhere in this work.

Bernard knew that the most important change in one's life was to convert to a single-mindedness, a "God-mindfulness." Turning one's heart and mind ever closer to God's mind and heart was the constant challenge of the monk—and every Christian. Bernard preaches time and again that we are to take God at God's word and to trust God.

Saint Bernard's ideal was—and is—that, at every mindful moment, we are to turn to God alone—not ourselves, not even to our friends (as much as they can help us). And the only true test of our faithfulness is to ask ourselves: Am I trusting in God—or myself or someone else? In his *Treatise on Love*, Bernard stresses the need to depend on God, to grow ever deeper in our dependence on God. Monasticism, Bernard knew, gets one out of one's own hands—and puts one squarely into God's hands. Daily this is reaffirmed in a monastic community, in the readings, in the prayers, in the teachings.

Writing about Cistercian life as the twelfth-century Abbot of Clairvaux, Bernard summed it up this way:

> Our way of life is abjection, it is humility, it is
> voluntary poverty, obedience, peace, joy in the Holy

Spirit. Our way of life means being under a master, under an abbot, under a rule, under discipline. Our way of life means applying ourselves to silence, being trained in fasts, vigils, prayers and manual labor; and above all it means clinging to that most excellent way which is Charity, and furthermore advancing day by day in these things and persevering in them until the last day.[1]

No, like the life of the U.S. Marines, this is not the life for everyone. (Shades here of "The few, the proud, the Marines"!) But neither is the life of you and me—the "everyday Christian"—for everyone. If we are to live it well, we are to live it with constant conversion, always beginning again.

What might motivate us to be faithful to our own version of the monastic life with all its demands on our time, energy and goodwill? Listen to the voice of Saint Bernard as he explains how he knew when Jesus was present to him in response to his own efforts to be converted:

He is life and power, and as soon as he enters in, he awakens my slumbering soul; he stirs and soothes and pierces my heart, for before it was hard as stone, and diseased. So he has begun to pluck out and destroy, to build up and to plant, to water dry places and illuminate dark ones; to open what was closed and to warm what was cold; to make the crooked straight and the rough places smooth, so that my soul may bless the Lord, and all that is within me may praise his holy name.[2]

Whatever the cost, isn't this the goal that all of us who bear Christ's name share? And who can live in today's world and not experience that hardening of heart of which Bernard speaks? We don't want it to happen. But it does. Our hearts become infected by the violence, greed, dishonesty and materialism that rear their ugly heads in the daily news.

We need the ministrations of Jesus, the tender of hearts. Listen once again as Bernard describes the consequences of our openness to "treatment" by the Divine Physician:

> Only by the power of the movement of my heart...did I perceive his presence; and I knew the power of his might because my faults were put to flight and my human yearnings brought into subjection. I have marvelled at the depth of his wisdom when my secret faults have been revealed and made visible; at the very slightest amendments of my way of life I have experienced his goodness and mercy; in the renewal and remaking of the spirit of my mind, that is of my inmost being, I have perceived the excellence of his glorious beauty, and when I contemplate all these things I am filled with awe and wonder at his manifold greatness.[3]

On the other hand, Bernard says he has no difficulty discerning when the Word has left him. His fervor for goodness dries up like a puddle on an August afternoon. His heart begins to cool off and harden once again. But our retreat mentor leaves us on this first day with a memorable example to follow.

> As often as he slips away from me, so often shall I call him back.[4]

For Reflection

- *Do you find yourself trying to work out your own conversion, instead of relying on God or family or spiritual companions? What will you do to rely more heavily on God? What daily prayer (for example, Thomas Merton's*

"Lord, I do not know where I am going..."; the Our Father)
can give you focus and serve this spiritual need?

- *What will you do to begin resolving your doubts about
  God's love for you, your worthiness, your destiny? What
  specific prayer that can help you do that (for, example,
  Mary's simple, "Let it be"; the psalms, such as Psalm 1,
  when in a quandary; Psalm 8, when you get down on
  yourself; Psalm 88, when you're lonely and frightened)?*

- *Our final reflection on each retreat day will be a reading
  from Saints Bernard and/or Benedict. As you listen to their
  voices, consider how you might integrate their wisdom into
  your daily life.*

On Jesus

Write what you will, I shall not relish it unless it tells
of Jesus. Talk or argue about what you will, I shall
not relish it if you exclude the name of Jesus. Jesus is
to me honey in the mouth, music in the ear, a song in
the ear.[5]

On Awakening

Let us then exert ourselves now. The Scripture
awakens us, saying: "Now it is the hour to arise from
sleep"; and with eyes wide open to the light of
heaven, and ears receptive to the word of God, let us
hear what his voice repeats to us every day. "Today if
you will hear his voice, harden not your hearts."[6]

Closing Prayer

Lord, help us see that change is good,
when it's change in your direction.
Teach us to be ever mindful of your way

as the right way,
the golden way,
the only way.
Teach us, Lord,
to trust in you,
as Benedict and Bernard trusted,
to trust that the grace to
endure,
the grace to flourish,
comes only from you.
Amen.

Notes

[1] Andre Louf, *The Cistercian Way* (Kalamazoo, Mich.: Cistercian Publications, 1983), back cover.

[2] Harvey Egan, S.J., *An Anthology of Christian Mysticism* (Collegeville, Minn.: Pueblo Books, The Liturgical Press, 1991), p. 174.

[3] Ibid., p. 175.

[4] Ibid.

[5] Ibid., p. 168.

[6] David A. Fleming, S.M., ed., *The Fire and the Cloud: An Anthology of Catholic Spirituality* (New York: Paulist Press, 1978), p. 65.

Day Two

A Vow to Live by a Code (The Rule/The Gospel)

Coming Together in the Spirit

Benedict and Bernard knew that the status quo just wouldn't cut it for themselves or their followers. They knew that a system was a better idea, albeit Benedict and Bernard each had somewhat different interpretations of the same system. Even Benedict's Rule was based to a large degree on an earlier rule, "The Rule of the Master," which Benedict adapted. Benedict never claimed that his Rule was totally original. Bernard and the Cistercians of old as well as modern Cistercians/Trappists have their own adaptations.

Our retreat directors both knew that we humans are creatures of habit, that there is solid value in repeated ritual and routine. "A time for everything under heaven" is more than just a quotable phrase for the Benedictines/Cistercians. And we can pick up on that beat.

Even more, we can pick up on the tenet behind all this: the tenet that "*regula*"—rule and regulation—are important for all humans, and especially for those who choose to walk a higher path.

Defining Our Thematic Context

You and I both know what it's like to be interrupted in the middle of something very important. People in monastic communities are always being interrupted. It's structured that way! There is not a monk or nun living in a monastery who does not know what it costs to abandon— for God's sake—their work, a conversation, a book, a ministry, a good night's sleep, to "have" to go to church for "Divine Office," for prayer time. Every monk and nun knows that "seven times a day," from Lauds right through to Vigils, one is called to interrupt one's own agenda for God's agenda.

Speaking of agenda, fully eighteen of the total of seventy-three chapters in Benedict's Holy Rule have to do with "prayer time"/the Divine Office. The monastic way is thus a liturgical way to holiness, a way that leads one to enter with one's whole being through the listening and chanting of the Word of God, and on through the eucharistic mystery. It is at prayer, especially communal prayer, that the community builds itself up and connects with the Divine.

The "every day" schedule of designated prayer times (the Divine Office) for the Trappist monks at the Abbey of Gethsemani begins with Vigils at 3:15 a.m. Other liturgical hours are interspersed throughout the day at six other appointed times, ending with Compline at 7:30 p.m. As you can see, this daily pattern of prayer requires a good deal of *disciplus*—discipline.

At other monasteries, the schedule may not appear as full or as rigorous. And yet, we all know it is not only what we do or how often we do it but *how* we do it (or even *why* we do it) that can matter so much.

Esther de Waal, who has written extensively on the Benedictine life, puts so much of this into perspective for us:

The Rule is simply to point me toward God and give me something to hold onto when I might otherwise be blown off course. So also with the vows, which always sounded so threatening when I knew little of monastic life, for the suggestions they carried of being negative, restrictive chains. But living with them has shown me something quite different. I have found that they offer me modes of perception, of seeing how I can handle my life wisely and creatively. They present to people outside of a monastic community, such as myself, three promises that together form one whole process.

They ask me to enter into a dynamic commitment that simultaneously holds me still (stability) and moves me forward (continual conversion) with all the time God, and not my own self, as the point of reference (obedience, listening intently). They have become tools for me, a most practical resource, which I sometimes think of as a survival kit, a lifeline that gives me practical help, not only to hold on to my relationship with God but also my relationship with others and myself.[1]

Opening Prayer

Lord,
guide my steps.
Show me the path
that leads to you.
Show me that you, too,
are right there on the path
with me, as well
as at the beginning
and end of the path.
For you are the God who is,
who was,

and is to come
at the end of the ages.
Amen.

Retreat Session Two
Taking the Via Media— *the Middle Way*

Benedict wanted to compose a Rule, a "way," that was not too hard, not too soft, but just right (a "Goldilocks" Rule!). He wished to ordain things so that "the strong would have something to strive after and the weak would not be driven away."

Benedict himself called the Holy Rule "a little rule...for beginners." And it is a little rule, with its total text barely more than nine thousand words (compared to perhaps three or four times that in this small book in your hands). But the Rule's brevity or simplicity shouldn't mislead us. For the Rule, says Esther De Waal, "has the moderation and compassion of the Gospel itself and it also has the urgency and the fire and passion of the Gospel."[2]

If the essence of Benedict's Rule were to be reduced to just two elements, the two might be cooperation and moderation. For Benedict, it was all about seeking the moderate or "Golden Middle" path to holiness—a path ordinary folks could take. But it was a path the basics of which had been mapped out years before in the Gospels. Benedict speaks of this in his Prologue to the Holy Rule: "Having therefore our 'loins girt about with truth,' and the observance of good works, let us, with the Gospel as our guide, go forward on his paths, that we may deserve to see in his kingdom him who has called us."[3] Indeed, Benedict's path, like Christ's path, is a path less traveled, perhaps. And yet it is a path traveled by many, a middle path, if you will, that asks only that we walk it by faith.

My brother-in-law likes to say that his basic rule to live by is: "Everything in moderation—including moderation!" He recites this with some good humor, but not unlike much of the Benedictine Holy Rule, there is paradox and contradiction in this saying. Tonight, as I write this, I am back at the Abbey of Gethsemani, and it has been some six months since I was here in this wonderful place. My very point is: Honest, I don't live down here in a Trappist monastery; rather, I have a family and three children and a dog, and I like to take a spiritual retreat here on a regular basis to keep myself in balance. I'm not out looking for another line of life or work—but a different angle on the life and work I already have. And, as a matter of fact, I've been here for about three days this stint, and I'm ready for a good pizza back home again with my little son, Patrick. (Moderation is one of my rules, too!)

I recently had this notion of the Benedictine "golden middle path" spelled out to me in sights and symbols most profound. I had the pleasure of visiting the Benedictine Abbey of Einsiedeln in Switzerland. There I joined the monks in choir beneath the baroque ceilings of their magnificent abbey church. True to the architectural style in which it was built, a 22-year restoration and renovation was just being completed. The results are spectacularly resplendent with ornate statuary, lavishly gilded trimmings, stained glass and polished brass to the hilt. I asked myself how Benedict would feel about this building. I think he would like it. Why? Because of what takes place in this extraordinary building and the monastery connected to it.

From Einsiedeln, Switzerland, I journeyed to Trappist, Kentucky, and the Cistercian Abbey of Gethsemani. The church there is stripped down, the bare, white walls and ceilings in starkest contrast with the decorous Abbey Church of Our Lady of Einsiedeln. And I ask myself: Would Bernard like this? Yes. (Very much. Bernard was not a fan of architectural magnificence. As a matter of fact, in 1127, Bernard wrote an *apologia* against artistic adornment, only to lose the battle in favor of more richly decorated churches, he himself admitting to the argument that if Christ himself were truly present at Eucharist, no sacrifice toward the enrichment of that moment was too great.) Would Benedict like this? I think so.

Why? Again, because the focus of both churches—and the communities of brothers who pray there—is on God alone, albeit in environments and interpretations most disparate. But both Benedict and Bernard had the vision to look beyond the surfaces—whether they be lavish or bare—and see what is really going on: Both churches are inhabited by households of God—living, breathing, worshiping families of God.

Most of all, Benedict and Bernard knew all about time and the sacredness of time. They knew that this was the precious commodity around which an austere and well-ordered life could best revolve. And while the Holy Rule of Saint Benedict gives many specific rules and regulations to observe, it teaches us in the largest perspective to honor not only creation but created time itself. By way of the Liturgy of the Hours, the Divine Office, the Church year and its liturgical seasons and cycles, we are to observe what Kathleen Norris in *The Cloister Walk* describes as "poetic time, oriented toward process rather than productivity."[4]

Benedict knew full well that if the greatest sins a Christian can commit are sins of omission or indifference, one of the best remedies was to punctuate time with reminders: with ringing bells as stopping points (not unlike the Eastern practice where the bell's ringing calls us to mindfulness); with Lauds or Matins or Vespers or Compline—all the "Hours" at prescribed hours of the day; repeated Psalm recitations that give the Christian "a center that holds." Just as the Psalmist "sets his soul at peace," Benedict's monks and we Christian followers of Benedict may set our souls by events made sacred by being marked and blessed in sacred time.

But even more important, Benedict does not have us join a monastic fellowship just to join in the activities on a daily or yearly calendar. Benedict has us participate in his Holy Rule in order to serve the Lord. *We don't come to a monastery or a church or prayers to follow techniques and methods and schedules (a Rule); we come to seek and find GOD.*

Putting Benedict's life and rule into perspective—for our everyday application—is Esther De Waal:

> The Church [in Benedict's time] was being torn apart by internal disputes.... In such a climate, as we well know, it becomes attractive to become inward looking, to cling to certainty, to establish barriers. But Benedict refused to do this. He remained a man whose mind was open, just as the doors of his monastery were always open, and as he wished his monks to have a heart open to all comers. His Rule is as a result a true *via media*, the middle way that holds centrifugal forces together to make them dynamic, life-giving. He holds together the emphasis on the solitary, on the withdrawal and disengagement that Cassian taught, with the emphasis from Basil on the communal or shared life. Here are the desert and the city juxtaposed. He speaks of the importance of both nature and grace. He is at once ascetic and humane. He is telling us these qualities are good and that we should be drawing on both.[5]

To paraphrase modern spiritual writer Frederick Buechner, speaking to us moderns: Neither the hair shirt nor the cashmere are fitting you today, my friend; what does fit is where your deepest gift and the world's deepest need intersect. For many of us that means the active life, for others of us, the contemplative; but for *most* of us it probably means something in between. Benedict's golden middle way is there for the taking.

One of my favorite illustrations of Benedict's understanding of our human need for this middle way is included in the Rule.

> We read that monks should never have wine, but nowadays they cannot be persuaded of this, so let us agree on this: that they should not go on drinking until they are full.[6]

Even Bernard agreed with such moderation. What he sought and taught was the same simplicity and *balance* of life that Benedict first espoused. Bernard's reforms brought the monastic life back to simplicity and away from overly elaborate and time-consuming rituals—not to mention the secular preoccupations—of the older style of monasticism.

When I think of Benedict and Bernard and their belief that "the middle way" was the best way, I am reminded of that great opening of the novel, *Robinson Crusoe*. Before Crusoe went astray and was deserted on an island for twenty-some years, his father advised him to choose "the middle state" in life, for it was "the best state in the world." How often, Robinson's father told his son, even kings lament their miserable high place in life; how often the poor curse their low state in life. But, oh, the many blessings and virtues of "the middle state":

> ...[T]emperance, moderation, quietness, health, society...; this way [the middle way] men went

silently and smoothly through the world, and comfortably out of it, not embarrassed with the labours of the hands or of the head, not sold to the life of slavery for daily bread, or harassed with perplexed circumstances, which rob the soul of peace, and the body of rest; not enraged with the passion of envy, or secret burning lust of ambition for great things....[7]

For Reflection

- What daily interrupters or reminders can you use in your life to bring God's care into your mind and heart on a regular basis? Example: A little prayer every time your child gets on or off the school bus. Or: Why not use the ringing of the phone as a spiritual signal to tune in to God for just that moment before you say, "Hello"?

- We tend to be black-and-white thinkers: "I'm a saint" or "I'm a sinner." "In church I pray" (saint); and then "When I get home I yell at the kids" (sinner). What about the middle ground? What about, as Benedict and Bernard suggest, "always beginning again"? Can we give ourselves permission to be seekers and not always perfect finders?

- What rules do you live by in your home? Are they the same rules your parents lived by? What gospel rules—especially the central rules about being faithful, hopeful and loving— are most clearly evident? How can you make them more evident?

- What is a realistic middle way for you to take in your spiritual life—a way that will work, day in and day out? You are probably not going to join a monastery (but then again, you might!); you are probably not going to get up an hour earlier each day to pray (but then again, you might!);

you are probably not going to join that Bible study group
that meets once a month (but then again, you might!); you
are probably not going to start being kinder to your spouse,
your children, your neighbor, your dog (but then again, you
might!).

On Making Spiritual Progress

To prefer nothing before the love of Christ.
To speak truth from the heart as well as the mouth.
Not to do an injury: but to bear one with patience.
Not to love much talk.
To use frequent prayer.
To hate nobody.
Not to be addicted to jealousy.
To avoid ambition.
To venerate the elders.
To love the younger.
To be reconciled to those who have quarreled with
    us,
before the sun go down. And never to despair of
God's mercy.[8]

Closing Prayer

Good and gracious Creator
of all that is good,
teach us to seek you
in "the golden middle"
of our very lives.
Teach us that
it is in balance and moderation
that we most serve you,
because that is where we
live the most.

May this middle way
center us
in you.
Amen.

Notes

[1] Esther De Waal, "Living With Contradiction: Reflections on the Rule of St. Benedict," *A Life-Giving Way: A Commentary on the Rule of St. Benedict* (New York: Harper & Row, 1989), p. ix.

[2] Ibid., p. xiii.

[3] *The Holy Rule of Saint Benedict*, ed. the Benedictine Monks of Saint Meinrad Archabbey (Saint Meinrad, Ind.: Abbey Press, 1975), Prologue.

[4] Kathleen Norris, *The Cloister Walk* (New York: Riverhead Books, 1996), p. xix.

[5] De Waal, p. xiv.

[6] Basil Hume, O.S.B., "St. Benedict: Ideas on Leadership," *Origins*, Vol. 26: No. 9 (August 1, 1996), p. 134.

[7] Daniel Defoe, *Robinson Crusoe* (New York: Airmont Publishing Company, Inc., 1963).

[8] David A. Fleming, S.M., ed., *The Fire and the Cloud: An Anthology of Catholic Spirituality* (New York: Paulist Press, 1978), pp. 71-72.

DAY THREE

A Vow to 'Bring Others Along' (Community/Hospitality)

Coming Together in the Spirit

One of the most powerful things community brings to individuals is courage—courage to be and do things we would never think of doing alone.

As the ancient monk Dorotheus observed, "I'd rather do things with others and have them come out wrong than do them by myself to make sure they come out right."

There's a story told that a certain visitor to a monastery asks the guest master: "Is that all the monks do here all day...nothing but pray?" Only to be answered, "Yes, but you have to admit it's pretty impressive when you see a whole bunch of us doing it at the same time."

The Cistercian constitutions and statutes refer to this "whole bunch" as a "community which forms a single body in Christ. Each brother is to contribute to the upbuilding of fraternal relations, especially by sharing with others the spiritual gifts he has received by God's manifold grace."[1]

Today, at the Abbey of Gethsemani, we are celebrating the Feast of All Benedictine Saints, November 13. In his second "Sermon for Saint Victor," our mentor Saint

Bernard reminds us that the saints continue to take an interest in us and do not forget our need for their intercession. Bernard says of Victor:

> No, he does not dwell in a land of forgetfulness or in a land of labor which keeps him occupied; it is no longer earth that is his dwelling-place, but heaven! And do you believe that the heavenly dwelling-place that welcomes souls is going to harden them, deprive them of their memory, or make them put aside their tenderness? Brothers [and sisters], the immensity of heaven widens the heart, it does not shrink it. It makes spirits joyful and not strangers to each other.[2]

It is this marvelous communion of saints that is our heritage and strength.

Defining Our Thematic Context

In a sense, it's all as simple as this: On our spiritual journey—the journey that really matters the most—we must resist the temptation to go it alone. The fact is: If we want to have life in Christ, we must have life within the body of Christ. That's family. And that's community.

One of the most wonderful things monasticism teaches us—and it's the same thing that any intense program of spiritual attunement teaches us—is this: "Thou shalt be aware." What this commandment means in the context of community is not the petty, mundane "Thou shalt be aware of thy sister's peculiarities, or thy brother's bad habits"; but rather, "Thou shalt be aware of the things that really matter." And community in Christ teaches us that.

> Gracious God,
> teach me that in "losing my life"
> I gain it.
> When I "lose myself" in community—
> even a community or a family or a church
> or a team or a committee or a class
> that is less than perfect—
> I become part of something much bigger
> than myself.
> I become a part of
> you.
> Amen.

RETREAT SESSION THREE
Community Makes Me Strong

Saint Bernard of Clairvaux is notorious for writing: "Community, my greatest penance." Not exactly the most inspiring words to start off this section all about community! And yet we must admit that in community we readily see the mediocrity of the human condition (not to mention the mediocrity of the person next to us in the pew, singing off-key!) There is no question that in community life—family life—minor irritants get magnified. We're simply with each other enough to really get to know each others' peculiarities.

But community in the Benedictine sense is not a club or a business relationship. Rather, it is the human face of the Church. And that means that while we are all one in the same Lord, we are also one very human family—a family that makes mistakes and argues and even sings badly! As Greg Friedman, O.F.M., puts it: "God entrusts the gift of faith to us in the 'earthen vessel' of human community. While we must always apologize for our shortcomings as Church, I believe that our human sin can never block God's work completely. Somehow, community continues to be the way God communicates, heals, and invites us to live more fully."[3]

Indeed, both Benedict and Bernard would overwhelmingly agree with Friedman's view—and the powerful conclusion about all of this put forward by the eloquent Walter Burghardt, S.J., in his book, *Tell the Next Generation: Homilies and Near-Homilies:*

> ...[T]his living, pulsing, sinning people of God, [I] love it with a crucifying passion. Why?
>
> For all the Catholic hate, I experience here a community of love. For all the institutional idiocy, I find here a tradition of reason. For all the individual repressions, I breathe here an air of freedom. For all the fear of sex, I discover here the redemption of my body. In an age so inhuman, I touch here rich joy and laughter. In the midst of death, I hear an incomparable stress on life. For all the apparent absence of God, I sense here the real presence of Christ.[4]

But how can we take this eloquence and apply it to our own everyday lives? Let's begin by applying it to the everyday lives of the monks in Benedict and Bernard's communities. Their apologia might go something like this: "For all his stubbornness and brashness, I see in Abbot Bernard a kind heart, deep down; for all the terrible personal grooming habits Brother Casimir possesses, I also see his generous spirit; despite the fact that Brother Terrence can't sing worth a hoot, I must admit he bakes a pretty good loaf of bread!"

And now to transfer this reasoning into our own families and communities: "For all the mediocre homilies I've heard Father Jim give, I also notice his visits to the sick are extraordinary; for all his total control of the TV remote control, I must admit Carl reads lovingly to the children at bedtime...." Etcetera!

It is in these everyday, minor conversions that full conversion of life for each of us begins to occur. And then, after and along with this *personal* conversion, it is a matter of assisting others, "bringing others along," as Bernard and Benedict would have it. But, you ask, knowing how hard personal conversion is: How can I bring others along? It's a formidable challenge, but both Benedict and Bernard give us guiding principles and lived examples.

Elsewhere in this book I cite the lovely quotation that goes something like: "A happy family is but an earlier heaven." Interestingly, the monastic cloister is often referred to as "the paradise of the cloister." While the image of monks and nuns living in blissful unity is a beautiful one—and a real one in so many ways, we can be assured—we must admit that the road chosen by monastics is long and difficult. Indeed, it calls for a fullness of love and mutual forgiveness that are absolutely extraordinary. In one of the most engaging passages of all to be found in the Holy Rule of Saint Benedict, we enjoy a portrait of the ideal community as Benedict dramatically sketches it. While Benedict's language is usually rather sober and matter-of-fact, here his pen is alive with emotion:

> Just as there is a wicked zeal of bitterness which separates from evil and leads to hell, so there is a good zeal which separates from evil and leads to God and everlasting life. This, then, is the good zeal which monks must foster with fervent love: they should try to be the first to show respect for each

other, supporting with the greatest patience one another's weaknesses of body or behavior, and earnestly competing in obedience to one another. No one is to pursue what he judges better for himself, but instead what he judges better for someone else. To their fellow monks they should show the pure love of brothers, to God loving fear, to their abbot unfeigned and humble love. Let them prefer nothing whatever to Christ, and may he bring us all together to everlasting life.[5]

Abbot Bernard, who himself was deeply molded in the Benedictine way, is noted for using a metaphor to describe community and one's application of this virtue. He spoke, in his Commentary on the Song of Songs,[6] of reservoirs and canals: "The man who is wise...will see his life more like a reservoir than a canal." Why? "The canal simultaneously pours out what it receives" while the reservoir "retains the water until it is filled [and] then discharges the overflow without loss to itself." Bernard was telling us to be reservoirs, of course, all of us receiving the love of God, holding on to it, letting it flow into every area of one's own life, and all the while letting it overflow into our family and community and all we meet!

Benedict and Bernard also had a lot to say about a significant aspect or by-product, of community: hospitality. In the Holy Rule, Benedict gives an inspiring entreaty to "treat all guests as if they were Christ himself." As usual, Benedict was taking a gospel imperative—in this case the dramatic Matthew 25 imperative—one of the conditions Jesus spoke of as a condition for our very salvation: "I was a stranger and you made me welcome."

Yes, hospitality is a true charism of Benedictinism— and I've seen it in action so very many times. If you have never visited a Benedictine or Cistercian/Trappist monastery, I would urge you to do so and see for yourself how guests are welcomed. I see this genuine welcoming almost daily at Saint Meinrad Archabbey as my coworkers and I eat lunch at the guesthouse. Frequently a monk or two is spending time with a visitor, very often a complete stranger, and the monk is explaining some element of the Benedictine life—or, better still, refilling the guest's coffee cup! It is also not at all unusual for the guest to be invited to join the monks "in choir," in their regular prayer services. As the Rule would indicate: "As soon as the guest is announced let the superior or some brethren meet him with all charitable service. And, first of all, let them pray together."[7]

My own favorite Benedictine hospitality story goes like this: In October 1996 I had the privilege of staying for a couple of days at the Abbey of Einsiedeln in Switzerland—as I've mentioned elsewhere in this book. What I didn't mention is that

- I was put up in a monastery guest room that was simple yet elegant and marvelously comfortable.

- The abbot himself came to join me at breakfast.

- Two young monks took me (and a Saint Meinrad monk-friend) out for wine and cheese at the "Saint Meinrad Gasthaus" at the top of a nearby peak.

At the *gasthaus*, as we were enjoying a glass of Einsiedeln wine, one of the monks asked, "In America, what is the name for this very thinly-sliced cheese? Isn't there a name you call it?" My American monk-friend and I came up with, "I guess we would call it 'shaved.'" Ah, said our host, lifting his glass of wine, "Then would you call this 'after shave'?"

That's hospitality!

For Reflection

- *There is a wonderful story about Abbot Bernard's human face and his love of God which dominated his life and overflowed into his community. It's taken from the book,* The Influence of Saint Bernard. *May it serve as a story for your own reflection on the real meaning of community:*

  Once when Bernard had completed the business which had taken him away from Clairvaux, he returned to the monastery and as soon as he could he went to see the novices.... [H]e soon found them all laughing with his easy and constructive talk, so that they would return with increased eagerness to the observance of holy obedience. But he called one of them to him and said, "My dearest son, what is this grief that is eating your heart out?" But the novice was too abashed to say anything. So Bernard continued, "Dearest son, I know what has been happening to you and with all the love I have for you as your father, I suffer with you...." When the holy father had said this, his words set the brother free from sorrow....[8]

- *Isn't it true that only a friend—a true friend—will come out and tell us some of the hard things about ourselves that we need to hear? And it is often only a real friend whose words we will believe and trust. Who is it in your family or community that you trust the most to humble you with some truth that could direct you better toward personal and spiritual growth?*

- *Can you recall how and where in community God has given you the gift of faith—or increased it? Perhaps through your parents who fostered your religious practices? Some friends at a youth or couples retreat? At a church service, or at a family meal where real sharing took place?*

- *Remember how in John's Gospel, Andrew is called first by Jesus, and then after Andrew comes to know Jesus, Andrew invites his brother Simon along. Bernard did much the same thing. Whom can you invite along for the journey?*

On the Community of Saints

Calling the saints to mind inspires, or rather arouses in us, above all else, a longing to enjoy their company, so desirable in itself. We long to share in the citizenship of heaven.... In short, we long to be united in happiness with all the saints.[9]

Closing Prayer

Loving God,
you teach us that when we Christians
come together
we somehow become greater than the sum
of all our parts.
Help me be mindful that even in my
prayer life I need to see—
as Benedict and Bernard did—
that communal worship
is a top priority, for it is in family/community
    that we see
the human face of the Church.
Amen.

Notes

[1] *Constitutions and Statutes of the Monks and Nuns of the Cistercian Order of the Strict Observance and Other Legislative Documents* (1990), p. 13.

[2] Charles Dumont, "Reading Saint Bernard Today," *Cistercian Studies*, Vol. XXII, 1987:2, pp. 170-171.

[3] Greg Friedman, O.F.M., in a *FaithNote*, "Community Makes Me Strong" (Saint Meinrad, Ind.: Abbey Press, 1991).

[4] Walter Burghardt, S.J., *Tell the Next Generation: Homilies and Near-Homilies* (Mahwah, N.J.: Paulist Press, 1988).

[5] *The Holy Rule of Saint Benedict*, Chapter 72.

[6] Ambrose Tinsley, O.S.B., *PAX: The Benedictine Way* (Collegeville, Minn.: The Liturgical Press, 1994), p. 54.

[7] *The Holy Rule of Saint Benedict*, Chapter 6.

[8] *The Influence of Saint Bernard*, p. 141.

[9] Saint Bernard of Clairvaux, "Let us make haste to our brethren who are awaiting us," *Christian Prayer: The Liturgy of the Hours* (New York: Catholic Book Publishing Co., 1976), p. 2053.

Day Four

A Vow to Work and Pray in Unity (Ora et Labora)

Coming Together in the Spirit

People were never made to stand alone. We need each other—and we need the Spirit's guidance—to help us walk the right paths. I've adapted the following story passed on by Anthony de Mello, S.J., in his *The Heart of the Enlightened*. It illustrates, in a humorous shorthand, the basic tenets of Benedictine life.

It seems that an eighty-five-year-old woman was being interviewed by a local reporter who wondered what advice she might have for others who had reached—or might someday achieve—that golden age. The birthday girl responded that daily prayer was an absolute necessity. In addition, she advised that people her age should find ways to make use of their talents and potential. "We need to be with others and, if possible, to earn our living by being of service to them."

The reporter could hardly hide the skepticism in his voice as he inquired, "And what exactly can you do for a living at your age?"

Said the woman, "Oh, I look after an old lady in my neighborhood."

That eighty-five-year-old woman may not have been a

Benedictine, but she and Saint Benedict would have hit it off very well.

Defining Our Thematic Context

So it is that *ora et labora* (prayer and work) are central tenets of the Holy Rule of Saint Benedict: "Then are they truly monks, when they live by the labor of their hands as did our fathers and apostles." And, as to prayer, he put it simply thus: "...we beg of God in prayer that His will may be done in us."[1]

We said earlier that the primary ministry of a monastic community is its prayer and worship: the Divine Office. And just what is the central thing that we see and hear going on during the Divine Office? Two words: glory and the cross.

For one thing, it is the monk's mission to testify that God is God; it is his duty to give thanks to God. And that means praising and giving *glory* to God. Thus you hear a hundred times in the monk's prayer-day: "*Glory* to the Father, and the Son...." "*Praise* to the Father and the Son...." Indeed, as the monks chant this doxology, they bow in deep reverence.

But Benedict is enough of a realist to know that all this praise is "work"; it is a task or service. It is, in a sense, symbolic of the cross that the monk bears over a lifetime of dedication and obedience.

One of the things I admire most about the monks I've had the privilege to know and learn from is this: They live by the *ora et labora* rule! (One Benedictine friend of mine loves to tell "the truth" about all of this though. Says he, with tongue in cheek, "Some days it's *ora* this...and *labora, labora, labora* that!") Indeed, even today monks find it necessary to support themselves and their community by the fruit of their labors. And they support and inspire us by their lifetime commitment to prayer, meditation and contemplation.

Opening Prayer

Lord, there are only a few things that matter
in our lives. You teach us what they are:
Love—closeness to you, the Father, the Son
and the Holy Spirit...
and closeness to one another,
the people we walk with
on our earthly journey.
While today we are blessed with so many riches,
keep us mindful that today—as every day—
it is only in the work of our hands and minds—
and in the prayer of our hearts—
that we can truly be rich,
that we can truly even survive,
and live with you.
Amen.

RETREAT SESSION FOUR
Holy Work, Holy Prayer— and Holy Play!

One of the most noteworthy aspects of the Holy Rule is its absolute and consistent attention to detail. I think this is no accident. This is where the monk lives; this is where God lives: in the ordinary details of life. And this is

Benedict's message to his brothers and to us. Throughout the Rule there are mentions of the bakery, the garden, the kitchen utensils and towels. (There is, in addition, this wonderful guideline to apply to the sale of crafts made by the monks—and now I see why Abbey Press books and gifts must be priced so affordably: "In setting the price of these things, let not the sin of avarice enter in; but let the goods always be sold somewhat cheaper than is done by men of the world, that in all things God may be glorified." Nice.)

How does Benedict encourage his monks to pray "enough"? He schedules their prayer times—down to the last detail. And while he emphasizes that prayer need not be long nor wordy ("In community, let prayer always be short...." Chapter 20) it must be contrite, fervent—and *regular*. How regular? "As the Prophet says, 'Seven times in the day I have given praise to Thee,' so we shall observe this sacred number of seven if at the hour of Lauds, Prime, Tierce, Sext, None, Vespers and Compline we fulfill the duties of our service" (Chapter 16).

And how does Benedict encourage his monks to pray "well"? The entire monastery environment is set up as a place, an atmosphere of prayer and reflection—from the usually remote location of the monastery itself to the architecture within it, from the beauty and order of the courtyard or garden to the observance of the Great Silence.

It is important here to emphasize that what Benedict was doing, and what Bernard and so many other abbots and monks who have come to follow the Benedictine way are doing, is only this: They are weaving *God* into the very cloth of daily life. One is never far from God, and God is never far from us. The entire daily program of official prayer-times are called the "Hours" or the "Divine Office." And, interestingly, the short midday prayer services are called the "Little Hours." Why? Because they're short. And yet they are necessary in order to keep God constantly in one's mind and heart.

But what, you might ask, is the point in all of this for us? And even if I applied the monks' "Divine Office" Hours to my daily life, wouldn't that take out all the spontaneity and personal-ness of one's prayer? Good questions. But consider: It is only through "practice, practice, practice" that good habits are acquired. And if our very days are punctuated, as the monk's day is, with regular reminders to practice and regular practice times, it's going to be very hard not to make progress.

The very word *contemplative* comes from two root words meaning to "make a temple with." The monk tries to make a temple with everyone and everything he contacts. Beloved writer Henri Nouwen used to say that "everything we meet is just waiting to be blessed," and unless we consciously bless the new day, the waking child, the visitor, the cup of tea or slice of bread, we're missing out on a whole dimension of life.

As to the *labora* (work) portion of the everyday formula, Benedict says this, in Chapter 48: "Idleness is the enemy of the soul. Therefore, the brethren should be occupied at certain times in manual labor, and at other fixed hours in holy reading." And here it is, in the middle of this chapter, that Benedict declares, "Let all things, however, be done in moderation...."

There is also this wonderful line in the Holy Rule— one not to be overlooked in monasteries...and in our homes: "On arising for the Work of God...quietly encourage each other, for the sleepy like to make excuses."

There is much debate today—as perhaps there has always been, on just how much and what kind of work a monk should really do. For example, Benedict of Aniane, a ninth-century Frenchman, maintained that since the world at his time had been converted, monastics should cease all mission activities and make flight from the world, akin to the hermit's, the whole of their existence. Then there are those who believe that the reason the Benedictines of the fourteenth century practically became extinct was that they failed to minister to the people out in the world around them. Living as "active contemplatives" is the balanced role most communities today strive for. While materialistic values are thus much abandoned, those in need of Benedictine ministries and witness are not.

Another interesting subject when it comes to monks and work is the issue of what *type* of work is "appropriate." Neither Benedict nor Bernard give terribly specific direction here—primarily because there was the clear understanding that manual work was a given; this was how a monastery was to survive and carry on. (There is, in addition, a long tradition of lay brothers—as opposed to the "choir monks" who did much of the everyday labor required to maintain a community; but even the choir monks were not exempt from manually earning their keep.) Thus farming, cooking, baking, cobbling, weaving, sewing, tailoring and shoemaking and so on, were a natural part of the monastic workday. In later ages, monks were to be better educated than the masses of people in society, and thus their work had larger ramifications for society—works such as educational and missionary work were deemed as important.

Some of the crafts and handiwork of monasteries have been legendary, and there has been a long tradition of excellence in monastic goods and creations—from pottery to liturgical vestments to cheese and fruitcake. There are many modern examples of types of work of such communities that derive their livelihood from the manufacture and sale of foodstuffs and the like. The Trappists at Gethsemani have for generations been known for their cheeses by mail, and their fruitcakes, and now a fudge with a hint of Kentucky bourbon inside. Then there are Trappistine fudges, embroidered goods, Benedictine jellies and jams and sausages. Saint Meinrad in Indiana for decades was in the sandstone quarrying business, not only for the construction of its own abbey buildings (and monks' tombstones) but also for many homes and businesses in surrounding communities.

Just how related to an apostolic work must monk-work be? One monk quipped that in order to make their cheese-selling "holy," they would need to open a franchise near Bethlehem and call it "Cheeses of Nazareth." (Sorry!)

The best answer that I think Benedict or Bernard or Jesus would give to this question of the type of work would be in the form of a larger question: How related to apostolic work must be the work of *any* Christian? And on this question, there have been long treatises and encyclicals and apostolic letters. To me, some of the best answers seem to be:

- Work that is work for the good of all.

- Work that has its proper place and proportion in our overall lives.

- Work that lets us use our best gifts from God and give them back to God and God's people.

(Monk Matthew Kelty at Gethsemani loves to tell tongue-in-cheek how jobs are assigned at Gethsemani Abbey. It goes something like this, and I'm paraphrasing: "We had a wonderful man who left the mortuary business and came to join us; the abbot named him head cook. Then we had a guy who was a terrific carpenter out in the world. He's the guy that puts the dried fruits into the fruitcakes. Why don't they have us doing what we're good at?... They should have me dancing!")

Finally, all of this *ora et labora*, this work and prayer,

are to be done in a *spirit of unity*. This doesn't mean it always has to be together at the same time and place—although for the most part it may be. Bernard, in his "Sermon on the Feast of St. Michael and All the Angels" pleads for this kind of unity in prayer and action:

> There are many things which please the angels, and which it delights them to see in us, like sobriety, chastity, voluntary poverty, repeated sighs of our desire for heaven, prayers accompanied with tears and with the heart truly directed to God. But above all these things, the angels of peace look to find among us unity and peace.... So let there not be divisions among us but rather let us all together form one body in Christ, being all members one of another.[2]

Adds Benedict, simply: "Let there be no strife, for all men are brothers."

Thomas Merton was quite a student of, and expert on, Bernard. As a matter of fact, some of Merton's earliest assignments from his abbot were to write about the doctors of the Church so as to make their thoughts more accessible to the modern monk as well as the rest of us.

In one of Merton's books on Bernard, called simply *Thomas Merton on Saint Bernard*, Merton gives us a good summary of Bernard's belief and teachings about work and prayer, action and contemplation. The tension that is always present between these two virtues was, as we know, very present in Merton's own life, as he constantly asked himself: What is "the better way...action or contemplation?"

Writes Merton:

> Although St. Bernard himself permitted Blessed Conrad to leave Clairvaux and live as a hermit, he ordinarily envisaged the contemplative life within

the ordinary framework of the community, and it was his characteristic task to show that a deep life of contemplation was possible side by side with its varied and numerous activities.[3]

Merton continues with an intense investigation and explanation of how he reads Bernard's view of this important question. He quotes Bernard's strong advice to his "wavering" monk, Eugene, later to become a pope: "Do not give yourself entirely to activity, and do not engage in active works all the time. Keep something of your heart and your time for meditation!"[4] However, Merton goes on to stress that the true life of contemplation is a call, and not to be taken by one and all, and not to be taken lightly. Indeed, Bernard (and Merton) advises strongly that one wait for this until God himself calls, and let him be very hesitant to interpret every interior "attraction" as an inspiration of the Holy Spirit! Merton goes so far as to quote the powerful saying of a Desert Father: "It is better to be fervent in a less exalted vocation than to be found tepid in a higher profession."[5]

What we are getting into here, speaking of this higher profession, of course, is mysticism. And even though Bernard was himself a mystic, he fully recognized he was only a part-time mystic. The rest of the time he had his feet firmly on the ground, and he recognized that most people operate that way, including most monks. "We inevitably fall back to our own level," as Merton summarized it.[6] But that's no excuse for not picking ourselves back up, again and again.

Both Benedict and Bernard humbly acknowledge this reality. And they recognize it as they both emphasize that one essential part of the *ora et labora* a monk does is *lectio divina*. What is meant by *lectio divina*? Why might I be interested in such an esoteric and difficult-sounding practice?

Well, literally speaking, *lectio divina* means merely *sacred*, or *holy*, *reading*. It is a type of reading that is a prayer in itself. No doubt you have experienced holy reading in your own life many times. It comes especially easily when one is reading poetry or great literature—or perhaps a book or magazine on gardening or nature or perhaps even sports! What happens is the reading inspires you, it lifts up your spirits by letting in the Spirit.

Indeed, this is a pretty lofty-sounding concept, and it is lofty. But Thomas Merton brings us back down to earth. He says that even Saint Bernard knew very well that the hidden meanings of Scripture reading—or any other reading, for that matter—were often more perfectly revealed to the monk meditating in the woods than the one studying in the scriptorium! No, neither Bernard nor Benedict (nor Merton) conceived of the contemplative life as a life of only study or scholarship. Rather, the contemplative life is to be a balanced life. And *lectio divina* is one of the balancing exercises prescribed.

Reading from Scripture is, indeed, a recommended part of the *lectio* regimen. One can hardly do better than to break open the Word of God, for when we can experience in our lives what we read in Scripture we become truly contemplative. When we read Scripture and such noble texts as the writings of the Church Fathers, the Desert Fathers and Mothers, the great poets and mystics and spiritual writers of previous times or our own times, we feed the inner spirit. The texts we read prompt beautiful and life-changing thoughts and insights. A ninth-century Benedictine abbot by the name of Smaragdus, summed up *lectio divina* this way: "Someone who wishes to be always with God must pray often and read often. For when we pray, we speak with God, but when we read, God speaks to us."[7]

Something else remarkably endearing about *lectio*

divina for us moderns is that it is really a "nonmethod" or a "nontechnique" in a world already too full of techniques and methods and gimmicks. The naturalness and flexibility of *lectio* will energize those of us already too burdened by mechanizations and things we already have to do.

While there are some time-tested guidelines and ideas that we may wish to seek out, there really is no rigid, universally adapted formula for practicing *lectio divina*, nor is there a set pattern or time limit for moving from one stage to another. Thus, in a sense, *lectio divina* perfectly embodies the Benedictine spirit of moderation and ordinariness, offering us moderns an ancient, traditional prayer exercise, all the while allowing us freedom to make it our own.

Finally, I called this section "Holy Work, Holy Prayer—and Holy Play!" So where does the play come in? Answer: It comes in community! (Back to the central theme of this whole book: "Seeking God Alone— *Together*.")

Although family/community life can be a mixed blessing, it has its moments of deep joy and thanksgiving and exhilaration. Whether the family size be two people or 902 (some monasteries actually used to be this large, though it appears that most are now somewhere on the range of a dozen to a hundred or so), each family or community has its own character, not to mention its own characters! When we spend our lives together, we find almost daily, if not more often, moments of laughter and fun and holy joy.

But first we would do well to hear the other side of the coin. Remember philosopher Jean-Paul Sartre's dismal line that "Hell is other people"? Then there's John Berchmans, a sixteenth-century Jesuit saint who is reported to have said, "My greatest mortification is the common life."

OK, now with that aside let's move on to the positive. First there is Psalm 133's wonderful declaration: "How good, how delightful it is for all to live together...." And then, what for me is the most profound and challenging and yet promising summary of the gift of community and the joy and achievement in it that I have read to date: a statement by Elizabeth O'Connor from her book, *The New Community*:

> ...[L]earning to be persons in community with other persons. This is the most creative and difficult work to which any of us will ever be called. There is no higher achievement in all the world than to be a person in community, and this is the call of every Christian. We are to be builders of liberating communities that free love in us and free love in others.[8]

To me this means being builders of *joy*, and one sure way to bring joy is to play. Some of my fondest memories of my seminary days at Saint Meinrad in the 1960's are not only of the student body at play, but the monks at play. Yes, the monks! And what a cast of characters they were. They had their serious side, but they also knew the value of play. I think of Father Hugh whose constant reminder to us out on the play fields was, *Mens sana in corpore sano*, loosely translated as: "A sound mind in a sound body." And then there were the other wonderful Latin word-plays we used to utter, truly words to live by! Sayings such as *Semper ubi sub ubi*, meaning: "Always where under where." And when heading out for the tennis courts, don't forget your *Decem est clamor*—"Ten is racket"! (And there were many more, but I'd prefer not to embarrass myself further—not to mention some of the monks who are now friends of mine in pretty high places!)

"Holy play" was always one of the unwritten

Benedictine rules for good community. You see it every day in your own family, where the saying runs so true that, "A happy family is but an earlier heaven." Ah, yes. All romantic views aside, it's work and prayer—and play—that make for the holy life.

Even Saint Bernard, who today is more remembered for his doctrine and his serious side, is also remembered as a person of joy. Interestingly, in the generation which followed his own, the written records indicate that the character trait most often stressed about Bernard, especially in monastic circles, was "his charm, his gaiety, and the joy which mingled both with his gentleness and his fervor. (After all, he was celebrated as a zitherist, and even described himself as a 'juggler.')" For me, it really helps to see this very human side of Bernard, a man who could stoop to playing the zither and juggled more than monastic kitchen assignments![9]

For Reflection

- *Do you count play or joy as an important virtue in your family or community? If so, how can you make it more evident?*

- *Is* labora, labora, labora *closer to the motto you live by? How can you make your life a more proper balance of work and prayer and play?*

- *While Benedict advised his brothers to "Keep death always before your eyes," he also said that our lives here on earth are temporary. How do you think that notion carries with it a message of freedom, a message that puts all the elements of our lives into perspective?*

- *Monasticism encourages a consistency of attitude: the same attitude or interior disposition in all that we do. In what practical ways can you keep yourselves mindful of this call to be God-centered in everything?*

On Invoking God

[Our] frequent needs oblige [us] to invoke God more often and approach him more frequently. This intimacy moves [us] to taste and discover how sweet the Lord is. Tasting God's sweetness entices us more to pure love than does the urgency of our own needs. Hence the example of the Samaritans who said to the woman who had told them the Lord was present: "We believe now not on account of what you said; for we have heard him and we know he is truly the Savior of the world."[10]

Closing Prayer

Gracious God,
may my work and my prayer
always be consecrated to you.
May I remember Benedict's wise advice that
"Whenever you begin any good work
you should first make a most pressing appeal
to Christ the Lord
to bring it to perfection."
Likewise, help me remember Bernard's
beatitude:
"Blessed are they,
Lord Jesus, for whom
you are ever the guide!"
Amen.

Notes

[1] *The Holy Rule of Saint Benedict*, ed. Benedictine Monks of Saint Meinrad Archabbey (Saint Meinrad, Ind.: Abbey Press, 1976), Chapter 7.

[2] Thomas Merton, *Thomas Merton on St. Bernard* (Kalamazoo, Mich.: Cistercian Publications, 1980), p. 150.

[3] Ibid., p. 35.

[4] Ibid., p. 48.

[5] Ibid., p. 50.

[6] Ibid., p. 53.

[7] Norvene Vest, *No Moment Too Small: Rhythms of Silence, Prayer and Holy Reading* (Kalamazoo, Mich.: Cistercian Publications, 1994), p. 63.

[8] Elizabeth O'Connor, *The New Community* (New York: Harper & Row, 1976), pp. 57-58.

[9] *Saint Bernard of Clairvaux, Studies Commemorating the Eighth Centenary of His Canonization*, ed. Basil Pennington, O.C.S.O. (Kalamazoo, Mich.: Cistercian Publications, 1977), p. 21.

[10] David A. Fleming, S.M., *The Fire and the Cloud: An Anthology of Catholic Spirituality* (New York: Paulist Press, 1978), p. 88.

*

DAY FIVE

A Vow to Be Humble (Obedience)

Coming Together in the Spirit

"Say nothing unless it will improve upon the silence" is a paraphrased saying of one of the Desert Fathers or Mothers. Similarly, writer Ernest Hemingway advised fellow writers: "Say only what you know about a subject—and then stop!" And finally, a current newspaper-cartoon character asks cynically: "What is it about 'Shut up' that you don't understand?" Humbling advice to those of us who speak and write for public consumption.

For me, the best lesson in humility came from my nine-year-old son, Patrick. One time, just after I had finished writing a book, I received a check from the publisher. That evening just before dinner I brought home the check to my family and proudly said something like: "Aren't you proud of me? Isn't it great to have a writer for a dad?" Patrick promptly responded, "Sure, Dad, but I'd be prouder if you were the pizza delivery man!"

Little Patrick, like Benedict and the Psalmist before him, recognized that people have gifts and talents, but service and obedience to the everyday needs of each other often must come first.

Another family story about obedience may ring true

for you. We have a dog, now two years old, who has twice attended what used to be known as obedience school. Why did the dog repeat obedience school? Because we didn't get it right the first time. Notice I didn't say the *dog* didn't get it right; *we* didn't. For the fact is that so much of *dog* training is really about people training.

What did Benedict and Bernard say about humility? Did they as abbots sometimes feel like their communities would gladly trade them in for "pizza delivery men"? You bet! But they also knew and accepted—even encouraged—this kind of thinking. In their very spiritual lives they both knew and acknowledged that they were *becoming* Christians, just as all of us are. We aren't there yet; we aspire to full Christian living, but it's difficult. Even in a monastery.

And even in a monastery one can relate to the old vaudeville line: "How do you get to Carnegie Hall? You practice, practice, practice." In our families the same rule holds so true: We need to practice, practice, practice humility and forgiveness. That can mean something as simple and humbling as changing the toilet paper roll when it runs out—yeah, you!—or forgiving another family member for *not* doing so! The ultimate key to all of this— as Benedict and Bernard and Jesus teach us—is to work on improving ourselves rather than to keep trying to improve the other person.

Defining Our Thematic Context

Earlier we spoke of a simple spiritual truth that we human beings come to know God through others, through the circle of community. And in order to serve the community and to serve God, we must free ourselves from self-centeredness. In order to accomplish this, we must practice self-forgetfulness; we must practice down-to-earth obedience.

According to the Benedictine constitution and statutes:

> By the vow of obedience a brother desiring to live under a rule and an abbot promises to fulfill all that lawful superiors command in accordance with the constitution. In thus renouncing his own will he follows the example of Christ who was obedient unto death, and commits himself to the school of the Lord's service.[1]

And what about Bernard himself regarding humility? Here is where he comes on strong! Indeed, Bernard's ego was tested often, as he was a person of enormous influence politically, both in Church and state in his time. Indeed, one of his "sons"— a monk from Clairvaux, that is—became Pope and took the name Eugene III. "What occasions and temptations to power this presented for Bernard!" Jean Leclercq tells us Bernard wrote to Pope Eugene: "It is said that you are not the Pope but in fact I am: great numbers of those who have affairs in court come to me from all sides."[2] Continues Leclercq:

> ...he had experienced the temptation to power. He knew the power of influence, success, even prestige and a dangerous glory. He suffered from this duality within himself: the monk vowed to total detachment, the contemplative called to seek God alone; and the man of action, involved in political affairs, with political obligations.[3]

While Bernard was aware of his gifts, he knew much of humility. In his Letter 372 to the Bishop of Palencia, Bernard

> develops the theme of gratitude one should have toward the Creator for the talents and graces which we owe him. But he adds that humility is not

inconsistent with a recognition of our own worth. On the contrary, it makes recognition possible. Humility is located on another, much deeper level. It is nothing other than the awareness of our need for God. Such is the truth of our condition: without God we can do nothing for God, and, since we are created for him, we cannot even be completely ourselves without him.[4]

In Bernard's own words, we read:

It is not enough to be subject to God, unless you are subject also to every human creature for the sake of God.... If then you wish to be perfect in righteousness, make the first step towards him who is less than you; defer to your inferior, show respect to your junior.[5]

What does all of this mean for us? It means being very forgiving people—*forgiving others for not being God*; forgiving *ourselves* for not being God! We human beings want and need so much, and when we expect all of this from our spouses or our children (or our dogs!) or our bosses or our teachers, we are bound to be disappointed time and again. So we have to keep on forgiving. *And, just as much, we have to seek forgiveness for our own faults.* That is the secret to humility.

Opening Prayer

O hope of every contrite heart,
O joy of all the meek;
To those who fall, how kind thou art!
How good to those who seek!
But what to those who find?
Ah, this no tongue nor pen can show;
The love of Jesus, what it is
None but his loved ones know.[6]

74

RETREAT SESSION FIVE
In Service to the Lord

In everything Benedict said and did, he showed that he knew the root of the word humility is the word *humus*, meaning earth. To be humble, to act or walk humbly is to act or walk in a down-to-earth, real, unpretentious way. Benedict's way is the humble, down-to-earth way to God. It can be our way, as well.

And the way is rooted in obedient service to the Lord. By that, we don't mean anything all that lofty—and certainly not a demeaning sort of philosophy that lets us tell ourselves we are no better than dirt. Rather, service to the Lord is rooted in the full realization that everything we have comes from God—and goes back to God.

Both Benedict and Bernard realized that the most perfect model of "the right kind of humility" was and is Jesus. Jesus went so far as "to humble himself to share in our humanity." Indeed, the Suffering Servant is a fine model for our suffering service to the Lord. In Jesus' obedience, even unto death, he showed us what is meant by true humility.

Benedict's most concise words on this theme are from the Prologue to the Rule:

> Listen carefully...this is advice from a father who loves you:... The labor of obedience will bring you back to Him from whom you have drifted through the sloth of disobedience. This message of mine is for you, then, if you are ready to give up your own will, once and for all....[7]

Benedict says a lot more about humility in his Holy Rule. As a matter of fact, his Chapter 7, entitled "Of humility," is one of the longest chapters in the Rule. Benedict talks about a dozen degrees of humility in all, comparing the degrees to the rungs on a ladder, taking us ever higher.

But it is Bernard who perhaps teaches us best about humility: His entire life was devoted to what he had discerned as the ultimate service to the Lord, namely, to bring himself and everyone he could get his hands on into following Christ—and preferably in a monastery, which is what he deemed as the ultimate "humbling" place, a place where God alone is the focus of one's will.

Bernard pushed all this a step further. One of his favorite dictums to his community members was: "Love to be unknown." This is reminiscent of Jesus' words in scolding the Pharisees that "Everyone who exalts himself shall be humbled, while he who humbles himself shall be exalted."[8]

How are we to humble ourselves for the sake of the Lord? How can we recognize that we are making progress in humility? My favorite homilist is Trappist monk Matthew Kelty. He answers this question of checking one's progress in humility by saying: "If you wonder if you're growing, check with your spouse. He or she knows. Check with your kids. They know. *And check with your dog.*"

Benedict would undoubtedly chuckle at Matthew Kelty's down-to-earth advice. The founder advised his sons to listen carefully to the opinions expressed by the youngest monks in chapter meetings "because God often reveals what is better to the younger."[9] Likewise, the author of the Rule instructed abbots to seek from visiting monks their observations about how the community was doing. Why? Because, Benedict said, "it is possible that the Lord guided him to the monastery for this very purpose."[10]

Anyone living in family/community knows this humility business is the toughest one of all. Practicing humility and forgiveness are lifelong exercises for families...at least until the kids are grown and gone and the dog dies (Erma Bombeck's definition of heaven!).

To bring this point home even more, a family therapist friend recently shared a cartoon with me. The cartoon showed a married couple, both sitting in a counselor's office and each wearing T-shirts that said: "I love me." The counselor is quick to say, "I think I see the problem here."

Bernard also warned his monks of a thing called "false humility." By this he meant a humility that keeps wisdom and holiness and good all humbly to oneself. This would be the gospel equivalent of having a light and keeping it "under a bushel" instead of sharing it with others. Bernard once admonished one of his followers for "the useless and damnable silence" in which we hold back the "good word that could be of advantage to many."[11] As we saw earlier, Bernard himself could not be accused of such a fault: When he believed in something he acted on it and evangelized everyone who would listen—plus, no doubt, many who didn't want to listen! Bernard thus saw it as a clear moral responsibility to not be too modest about sharing the faith.

One of my favorite modern mystical writers is Annie Dillard. As a matter of fact, in my mind her works would readily qualify for anyone's *lectio divina*. I would especially recommend her Pulitzer Prize-winning *Pilgrim at Tinker Creek*. It was Dillard who wrote with the passion, zeal and evangelism of a Saint Bernard of Clairvaux. See what she says about keeping something good to yourself:

> One of the few things I know about writing is this: spend it all, shoot it, play it, lose it, all, right away, every time. Do not hoard what seems good for a later place;...give it, give it all, give it now.... *Similarly, the impulse to keep to yourself what you have learned is not only shameful, it is destructive* [italics mine]. Anything you do not give freely and abundantly

becomes lost to you. You open your safe and find ashes.[12]

Hardest of all our sins to remember are our sins of omission. After all, we "didn't do anything." And that can be the problem.

For Reflection

- *The monk or nun sees the will of God in the will of the superior. We may forget that we, too, take a vow of obedience and humility. In the Sacraments of Baptism and Confirmation, Catholics make some pretty firm promises in this regard. Take time to privately review these commitments.*

- *Does false humility keep you from spreading the Good News? What do you know about the spiritual life that you can share for the benefit of others?*

- *Conversely, do you, like me, find it hard to let the other person have his or her "say"? Do you find it almost impossible to just listen? Today—at a meal, a meeting, a prayer time—humbly vow to just listen, to hear a piece of Good News coming from another person. (Tomorrow you can talk again!)*

- *Matthew Kelty says that a monk "makes a quiet investment in wonder." The monk isn't compelled to create wonder but to humbly receive it. Take time today to simply marvel, muse or wonder fully in the work and wonder of others, in the work and wonder of God.*

On Flowing Into God's Will

As a drop of water seems to disappear completely in a big quantity of wine, even assuming the wine's taste and color; just as red, molten iron becomes so much like fire it seems to lose its primary state; just as the air on a sunny day seems transformed into sunshine instead of being lit up; so it is necessary for the saints that all human feelings melt in a mysterious way and flow into the will of God. Otherwise, how will God be all in all if something human survives in [us]? No doubt, the substance remains though under another form, another glory, another power.[13]

Closing Prayer

Loving and merciful God,
this "humility" thing always puzzles me.
It's so hard for me to know the difference between
evangelizing and "butting in,"
between being rightfully proud of my gifts
and being arrogant about them,
between being "obedient" and being
foolishly submissive.
Through the intercession
of Saints Benedict and Bernard,
teach me to be "down-to-earth"
enough in my words and deeds,
but also "lifted up" enough in my
intentions.
Amen.

Notes

[1] *The Constitution*, p. 10.
[2] Jean Leclercq, O.S.B., *Bernard of Clairvaux and the Cistercian Spirit*

(Kalamazoo, Mich.: Cistercian Publications, 1976), p. 56.

3 Ibid., p. 68.

4 Ibid., p. 76.

5 Basil Pennington, O.C.S.O., *Saint Bernard of Clairvaux*, p. 110.

6 Bernard of Clairvaux. "Jesus, the Very Thought of Thee," a hymn which may be found in Richard J. Foster's *Devotional Classics* (San Francisco: HarperSanFrancisco, 1993), p. 45.

7 *The Holy Rule of Saint Benedict*, ed. Benedictine Monks of Saint Meinrad Archabbey (Saint Meinrad, Ind.: Abbey Press, 1975), Prologue.

8 Luke 18:14b.

9 *The New Dictionary of Catholic Spirituality*, ed. Michael Downey (Collegeville, Minn.: The Liturgical Press, 1993), p. 85.

10 Ibid.

11 *Thomas Merton on St. Bernard* (Kalamazoo, Mich.: Cistercian Publications, 1980), p. 67.

12 Annie Dillard, "Write Till You Drop," *The New York Times Book Review*, May 28, 1989.

13 David A. Fleming, S.M., *The Fire and the Cloud: An Anthology of Catholic Spirituality* (New York: Paulist Press, 1978), p. 90.

DAY SIX

A Vow to Seek Simplicity (Poverty and Chastity)

Coming Together in the Spirit

A monk-friend of mine tells me that a monk isn't supposed to require all kinds of flashy surroundings. Rather, a monk is supposed to develop an "inner geography," a beautiful *inner* landscape.

In his excellent audiotape *Landscapes of the Sacred*, Bishop Robert F. Morneau describes both the external and internal geography of the Carmelite poet Jessica Powers. She spent forty-seven years in the Carmel of the Mother of God in Milwaukee, Wisconsin (her external geography). Her much more important internal geography (moral, psychological, spiritual life) is revealed in her poetry.

One of her poems, "The Place of Splendor," speaks of the inner landscape through which the believer travels to meet God in the soul. She writes:

> The steps lead down
> through valley after valley, far and far
> past the five countries where the pleasures are,
> and past all known
> maps of the mind and every colored chart
> and past the final outcry of the heart.

No soul can view
its own geography; love does not live
in places open and informative.[1]

This is the beautiful inner landscape of which my monk-friend spoke. And only those who practice simplicity can journey there.

Defining Our Thematic Context

Monks did not invent simplicity and order, no more than they invented God. But monks are expert at—and committed to—seeking simplicity and order and God. Nor does one need to be a great artist like M. C. Escher to agree with him that "Simplicity and order are...certainly the most important guidelines for human beings in general."

Much of Benedictinism and Cistercianism is about simplicity and order. But it is also about giving and not getting (in the Western sense of the word "getting"). In the spiritual sense, one gains all by losing all, of course. "Seek first the kingdom of God and all will be given to you." "He who would save his life shall lose it; he would lose his life shall save it."

So in this section we will be talking about renunciation, about giving things up in order to gain something greater. It's about holding on to nothing beyond the necessary.

What do Benedict and Bernard demand that followers of Christ give up? For the monastic follower, the monk, he or she is asked to give up such things of the world as:

- Freedom (Example: If I'm in church five or seven times a day, I'm probably not going to be free to go golfing this afternoon.).

- Family (the traditional family, of course).

- Sexual joys (but not sexuality).

- Steak dinners (or meat entirely in some religious orders).

- A long list of material things.

- Power and authority.

Indeed, the monk lives in a *cloister*—literally, from the Latin word *claustrum*, meaning a "shut-in place." And what is "shut in" with the monk? An inner geography without much adornment—except for the beautiful inner landscape one develops when God is shut in with you!

Opening Prayer

> Lord, let me realize that
> while I know I need to "look up" to see you,
> I also need to "look down" here on earth,
> lest I stumble and fall.
> I remain only a stranger,
> passing through my life,
> until I dig down,
> dig in,
> and find you
> in the commonplace,
> in the everyday,
> in the simplicity of
> now.
> Amen.

Keeping Life Simple

When one thinks about it, Benedictines are cultural revolutionaries. Their very actions (and inactions) are like treasonous acts against a culture of unbridled profit-making and productivity.

Perhaps "revolution" sounds like too dramatic of a word. And yet perhaps it is an appropriate term. Ironically, the simple antidote to our confused and sometimes misdirected (or undirected?) lives is simplicity itself. Or call it ordinariness. For this is the key to this whole thing called Benedictine spirituality, and it is the key to a wondrous life in Christ.

How can you and I join the Benedictine revolution toward simplicity? The "revolutionary" insight is that Benedict insisted that no moment in the day is too small for the nearness of God. We need not look for anything terribly dramatic or heroic when we look for God. Rather, Benedict (and Bernard and so many after him) urged would-be followers of Christ to simply engage the everyday stuff of life. That's where God is actively present, participating in our lives: in the breaking of the bread as well as in the making of it. God is a God we can connect with, not a God so far away as to be unreachable.

How do you and I connect with this loving God? By being pray-ers and lovers. And I can think of no better or simpler way than to use the very tools that monks have been using for hundreds of years: the psalms. When I go on retreat at the Abbey of Gethsemani, I am invited into the monks' psalm prayers. (The vast majority of all the official community prayers recited or sung at any of the "Hours"—whether it be at 3:15 a.m. Vigils or 7:30 p.m.

Compline—are psalm prayers.)

Benedict and Bernard revered the psalms. Why? Because the psalms represent the simple prayer of every one of us. All the "hours" in the Liturgy of the Hours except the first begin with the incantation: "O God, come to my assistance. O Lord, make haste to help me." You can't get simpler—or more direct than that!

And always each psalm is concluded with the "doxology." At Saint Meinrad, the Indiana Benedictine monastery, it goes this way: "Glory to the Father, and the Son, and the Holy Spirit; as always before, so now, and evermore. Amen." At the Trappist (Cistercian) Abbey of Gethsemani it goes like this: "Praise to the Father, the Son, and the Holy Spirit, both now and forever, the God who is, who was, and is to come at the end of the ages. Amen."

And what is "in-between" the opening incantation and the closing doxology? A beautiful, powerful pattern of psalms, selected from the complete Old Testament Book of one hundred and fifty Psalms. There are praising psalms, angry psalms, pleading psalms, thanksgiving psalms, joyful psalms, quiet psalms and loud psalms. The psalmist was trying to tell God something. Benedict and Bernard were trying to tell their monks something—and us, too.

Bernard was quite specific on just how the psalms were to be chanted:

> If there is chant, let it be very solemn, not harsh or wanton. Let it be pleasant, without being light, that it may charm the ear and thus move the heart. Let it alleviate sadness, let it calm anger. Let it not drain the text of its meaning, but make it fruitful.[2]

One older monk-friend tells me that although he has prayed certain psalms many, many hundreds of times with his brothers over the years, "sameness" is never a problem—because while God is the same, he himself is never the same as the last time he recited or sang the psalm.

As a matter of fact, contends my monk-friend, these psalm-prayers—and all our prayers—are about something much more profound than just words; they are about *relationship*. And as anyone involved in any relationship knows, there can be much communication without words. Sometimes just presence is enough.

Yes, in a monastery the psalms are chanted in community, by monks in choir—another reminder that life is essentially communal, interconnected, relationship-centered.

And now, to go beyond the psalms and our more formal prayer life, what can you and I do out here in the world to emulate Benedict and Bernard's wisdom on living more simply?

Let's hearken back to the last chapter's theme of humility, which is so related to the theme of simplicity. More specifically, let's look at Chapter 7 of Benedict's Rule, "Of humility," and apply the simple wisdom there to our daily lives. Benedict refers to the twelve degrees of humility. He uses the symbol of a ladder with twelve rungs that the serious God-seeker aspires to climb. "The ladder itself...is our life in the world.... The sides of the ladder we declare to be our body and soul, in which our divine vocation has placed divers rounds of humility and discipline which we must ascend."[3]

The first degree of humility is to keep the fear of God before one's eyes. Benedict goes so far as to refer to the fires of hell as well as the rewards of heavenly life as motivations for keeping all in perspective. You can't get much simpler than that. Even though it is less in vogue today to reduce everything to the black and white of a heaven or a hell "pay-off" in the end, we would do well to reduce life to its essence and remember that we are to live in love and will be ultimately judged by our love. It is love that matters—and lasts. Practical application: Speak your love to someone (or Someone) today in some simple way, or with the simplest of words: "I love you."

The second degree of humility is that we are to love not our will, but God's will, to emulate Jesus himself who said: "I have come not to do my own will but the will of the one who sent me." Practical application: Speak the simple words of the "Surrender" prayer of Thomas Merton, as he interprets this Benedictine plea for simplicity: "Lord,...the fact that I think I am following your will does not mean that I am actually doing so. But I believe that the desire to please you does in fact please you."

The third degree of humility is simply that one obediently submit to one's superior. Who is your superior? If that's at all hard to answer, as it might be, we do well to simply remember that God is our ultimate superior. Trappist Father Jacob Raud likes to put his humble prayer this way: "Who loves me? God. What do I need? Nothing. What do I have? Everything." This can be our prayer, too.

The fourth degree of humility is to be patient in adversities. For the monk that might mean something as simple as forgiving the monk next to him for arriving late to choir; for you and me it might mean intentionally stopping to smell the roses, at the risk of being late, even though our culture always insists we have to hurry.

The fifth degree of humility is to confess our sins and shortcomings. Practical application for us seekers of simplicity: Acquiring the simple habit of saying "I'm sorry," and passing on this habit to our children and others by our example.

The sixth degree of humility is that one be content with "all that is mean and poor." Brother David Steindl-Rast, O.S.B., contends that the happy people are grateful because they got what they like. While in reality the grateful people are happy because they like what they got. One practical application for us: Unplug the TV or computer and get into an hour of *lectio divina*, especially reading and praying over the Beatitudes.

The seventh degree of humility is that one recognize and openly declare oneself "unworthy." Practical application: Take out the garbage instead of pushing someone else in the household to do so! Or: Create less garbage by buying fewer over-packaged goods.

The eighth degree of humility is to be "of the house" and follow the "house" rules. This very down-to-earth rule suggests to me, among other applications, this practical, absolutely simple yet absolutely difficult one: Spend some time with those I love.

The ninth degree of humility is to respect silence. Practical application: Need I say *anything*?

The tenth degree of humility is not to be "too easily moved or quick to laughter." Gosh I hate this one! But I think the essence of this is to recognize that our spiritual lives are pretty serious stuff indeed. If I laugh too readily or give in to the tendency to be witty or clever instead of listening and hearing, I'm at fault. Practical application: Turn off a sit-com, any sit-com! Or: Vow to really listen during the next conversation you're engaged in.

The eleventh degree of humility is to speak gently. To me this means to demonstrate respect to all in one's company, to show reverence and recognize that one's words as well as the delivery of those words has an impact on others. Practical application: Speak gently and carry no stick!

The twelfth degree of humility is to show one's humility to all. This speaks to me of being true to one's self, being oneself, and not trying to communicate some false image or identity. Practical application: Be like

Thomas Merton who was once confronted in a public place by a stranger who asked, "Aren't you Thomas Merton, the famous Trappist writer?" Replied Merton: "I'm a Nelson County farmer."

We haven't said much about poverty and chastity— and yet we've said a great deal about them. But there's more.

Let me begin with a funny story a monk-friend likes to tell. (He will remain anonymous, as will the particular monastery!) The story goes that every monastery needs to be about the business of recruiting new monks. And in many ways this gets tougher and tougher in our secular society. But one day a prospective recruit shows up at the monastery and, true to the Benedictine charism of hospitality, is warmly welcomed. He is chauffeured around the monastery grounds in a shiny new car; he's presented with a lovely keepsake at the monastery gift shop; at dinner he is lavishly served a fine dinner at the head table with the abbot and prior; and all this is followed by a nice after-dinner drink in the monastery recreation room.

Finally, as it is time to go, the young recruit is asked if there is anything more he'd like to do or see to help him with his decision. "Yes," replies the young recruit, "If this is poverty, show me chastity!"

Ah, poverty. Ah, chastity. In our culture they both seem totally out of vogue. We don't even fully understand their true definitions anymore. In the case of poverty, perhaps it is just as well that we equate poverty with this terrible thing where people don't have enough to eat or a place to live. While most of us are blessed with not being able to understand what this must be like, we strive to be conscious of its existence and to help eradicate it from society. But there is also a "good" poverty—a virtuous poverty that has one asking again and again throughout life: Do I really need this? Is more really better? This is the kind of consciousness and austerity and "good poverty" that Benedict and Bernard taught. (And, not too far away, "in another part of the forest," Francis of Assisi was to go all the way and make a lover out of *Lady Poverty*—or was it that Lady Poverty made a lover out of him?)

With regard to chastity, too, the tendency is to equate chastity in our society with sexual naïveté rather than with discretion or valor or virtue. We may not even think that one facet of chastity is fidelity. The ideal that Benedict and Bernard espoused was a chastity that allowed one to be focused and *faithful*. It is easy to throw out words like "detachment" and "distraction" and "purity," and what chastity is *not* when discussing the virtue of chastity. But what *is* it? It is a faithfulness that allows for a devotion and intimacy beyond human understanding.

Listen to Bernard in his response to that ecstatic paean to love, the Song of Songs:

> Only the touch of the Spirit can inspire a song like this, and only personal experience can unfold its meaning. Let those who are versed in the mystery revel in it; let all others burn with desire rather to attain to this experience than merely learn about it. For it is a melody that resounds abroad by the very music of the heart, not a trilling on the lips but an inward pulsing of delight, a harmony not of voices but of wills. It is a tune you will not hear in the streets, these notes do not sound where crowds assemble; only the singer hears it and the one to whom he sings—the lover and the beloved.[4]

How did Bernard and Benedict achieve this burning desire for passionate unity with God? Poverty, chastity, simplicity. Living in what we would term countercultural ways. We, too, are to embrace an "alternative" life-style— one that is not based on money or power or promotion or lust or greed. Conversely, this is not to say that Benedict didn't "get real." He was a realist if he was anything, and his Rule shows a deep and touching humanity in these issues. For him, spiritual growth was not simply an intellectual concept; it was something that was bound up in the flesh and bones of human strengths and failures. Clearly there is a place for the material things in life, but with it an uncompromised bias toward the poor, the sick and anyone in need of protection.

In the area of sexuality and intimacy, it appears we all still have a long way to go. And yet Benedict's ultimate point on this issue was: intimacy with *God* first and *God* last and *God* in between. The emphasis is on sacrifice—a death to the self—for the sake of the Other. Contemporary theologians have much to say about this "death to self" for the sake of another, regarding love and intimacy and sexuality. And the answers aren't always a list of thou shalt *nots*. Even Benedict, in Chapter 2 of his Rule, quotes the saying of Jesus in Matthew (6:33) on "seeking first the kingdom of God." Jesus did not say seek *only*, but seek *first*.

What much of this boils down to is the question of just how literal we should be in interpreting Benedict's rules. Better: Just how literal should we be in interpreting Jesus' "rules" in the Gospels? The interpretations can be pretty subjective, and they probably ought to be on some things. Questions about how much sacrifice is required in my life need to be very personal questions with very personal responses in order to give them merit. The Cistercians throughout the ages have been classic at debating and interpreting these "How much?" questions. One clear result is that there is a Cistercian Order of the *Common* Observance and a Cistercian Order of the *Strict* Observance.

Is one order better than the other? It is as simple as

asking: Is more sacrifice better than some sacrifice? Not really. There are no simple answers. If in our families we insisted that all of us pack up and go to Mass every morning and then go to a monastery in the evening for Compline and then keep total silence all the way home, that would be a sacrifice for sure. But would it be better in the long run than weekend Mass and an occasional weekday Mass and a reminder to the kids to say their night prayers? Not for my family, it wouldn't. But maybe for yours it would be. While Benedict and Bernard imposed limits and restrictions and prescribed much of the community members' sacrifices, they were not starry-eyed idealists who didn't know there were reasonable limits to any sacrifice. But they did know that sacrifice needed to be a big part of the Christian life.

But what is a sacrifice for me may not be a sacrifice for you. (I can exercise a good deal, but don't cut back on my food supply!) I love the way Benedict emphasizes individuality within his family of monks. Benedict recognizes that we are all not made out of the same mold. Some monks are docile, some not; some intelligent, some not. It follows, therefore, that some monks will learn by teaching and others by example. Though, just as in families, no favoritism may be shown, each person and personality must be treated uniquely. This is pure Benedict. Coax one, scold another; encourage this one, reprove that one. Great family psychology here.

A final word about the Benedictine way of keeping life simple. And that final word is: *pax*, that is *peace*. Benedict and Bernard, like Jesus, call us to peace. And monasteries, if they are anything, are centers of peace, peace institutions that mark themselves in stark contrast to a world which stresses blind production, making money, making things, making war. The Christian monastery is one of the few places dedicated to the development of professional peacekeepers. Oftentimes the sense of peace in a monastery absolutely hits you in the face (to use a non-peaceful image!) the minute you set foot on the grounds. "They are to pray together," wrote Benedict in his Rule, "and thus be united in peace." Further, upon our sharing in the monks' Divine Office, the psalm chants, the monastic environment itself, one may indeed experience a peace that surpasses all understanding.

Peace is the objective of all of the "soul work" of the monk, the spiritual seeker. (That's you and me!) And just what are the simple things in life? A short list, for me, might begin with "monk things" like:

reading

music

sunset

gardens

birds

walking

quiet conversation

painting

baking

But it would need to go beyond "monk things" and get into simple things like:

a game played with a child

a convertible or bicycle ride

listening to an Elton John song

walking the dog

watching a movie

making pancakes

sitting on the porch

flying a kite

Name your own "monk things" and enjoy the process.

For Reflection

- *Do you find yourself waiting for bolts of lightning to outline God's face? What are some of the simpler, more commonplace places to seek the face of God?*

- *"After enlightenment, do the laundry" is the glib admonition of one Zen teacher. Benedict and Bernard might say, "Do the laundry and be enlightened." Do either of these theologies work for you? If not, spend a little time writing one that does work.*

- *What is your favorite psalm? Can you recall how you felt the first time you read a psalm that addressed God with such honesty and no-holds-barred directness? Describe your response.*

- *Benedictines have been accused of raising inefficiency to an art form. ("Interrupting" their lives and going to church to pray six or seven times per day; "building in" silent periods into the middle of prayer services when instead everyone could be going their way doing something more productive.) Are we sometimes so determined to be efficient that we lose sight of what true effectiveness is in the life of the spirit? How will you make your own life simpler and less efficient?*

On Seeking the Kingdom

There is no doubt that [God] will assist us willingly
in time of need, since he helps us so often in time of

plenty. It is written: "Seek first the kingdom of God and his justice, and the rest will be added thereto." Without being asked, he promises to give what is necessary to [the one] who withholds from himself [herself] what he [she] does not need and loves his [her] neighbor. This is to seek the kingdom of God and implore his aid against the tyranny of sin, to prefer the yoke of chastity and sobriety rather than let sin reign in your mortal flesh.[5]

Closing Prayer

Lord,
what we seek is you;
what we seek is to live more constantly
and more intensely
in your presence.
Show us how to live
mystically
every day.
May we "prefer nothing
whatsoever to Christ."
Amen.

Notes

[1] *Selected Poetry of Jessica Powers*, ed. Regina Siegfried, A.S.C., and Robert F. Morneau (Kansas City, Mo.: Sheed & Ward, 1994), p. 123.

[2] Jean Leclercq, O.S.B., *Bernard of Clairvaux and the Cistercian Spirit* (Kalamazoo, Mich.: Cistercian Publications, 1976), p. 20.

[3] *The Holy Rule of St. Benedict*, Chapter 7, "On humility."

[4] Quoted in *Living With Contradiction: Reflections on the Rule of St. Bernard*, by Esther De Waal (Harper and Row, San Francisco, 1989).

DAY SEVEN

A Vow to Remain Faithful (Stability)

Coming Together in the Spirit

Just as the psalms are expressions of the simplicity we seek, so are they expressions of stability. Look at it this way: If it's 7:30 at night in the spring of 1962 and Brother Chrysogonous is celebrating with great joy his entry into the order, he sings with the choir: "I lie down to sleep and peace comes at once for you are my God" (Psalm 3:6); and if it's the winter of 1992 and Brother Chrysogonous is dying of cancer and he knows it but can still shuffle into the choir stalls at 7:30 p.m., he will sing: "I lie down to sleep and peace comes at once for you are my God."

It's called stability. And it's called fidelity or faithfulness. And it's what all of us are called to.

Thomas Moore, author of the best-selling *Care of the Soul* and *Soul Mates*, writes about this solid, unyielding sense of monkish stability in his book *Meditations: On the Monk Who Dwells in Daily Life*. He uses the monastic singing of chants in choir as a symbol for this stability:

> As monks sing their chants they are making music
> that mirrors and models the life they are living.
> Chant is modal. It doesn't have the drive toward
> ending or the insistent relationships between notes

and chords that modern music has.... In a modal life, endings are soft, peaks are rounded, and energy is reserved. Modal life, like modal music, has the special beauty that comes with the absence of drivenness.[1]

Defining Our Thematic Context

We who are often afflicted by "drivenness" do not belong in a monastery. But, by our very humanness, we can profit from the mentoring of Benedict and Bernard. As one observer says, "Nevertheless, at the heart of the Rule is a core of truth about the human condition. It contains a series of brilliant insights concerning how one may make ordinary life into something deeply fulfilling."[2]

How can deep fulfillment be found in simply "staying put"? Further, can *we* "stay put"? Our culture tells us to look, dig, uncover, search, *move* constantly! What I firmly believe we can do to apply this virtue of stability to our own modern, nonmonastic lives can be boiled down to one word: availability. I believe availability to God is "the spirit of the law," this Benedictine rule of stability. What do I mean by this? I mean that we give God a clear and continuing message that says simply, "You know where to find me. Here I am. I'm available." These are the constant messages a monk sends to God. So can we.

Opening Prayer

Lord,
I know that saying yes
to you
means saying no

to a lot of people and
places and things that are
not you.
Strengthen my resolve
to say my yes
and to do my
yes
to you.
Amen.

RETREAT SESSION SEVEN
'To Prefer Nothing to the Work of God'

There is a story of a hermit called Martin who lived
not far from Saint Benedict's monastery. In order for the
hermit to make certain he would not abandon his cave, he
bound himself to the rock with an iron chain. When
Benedict heard of this, he admonished the hermit by
sending him this message: "If you are a true disciple of the
Lord, you would do better to bind yourself to Christ."[3]

So Benedict brings it back to Christ. Always back to
God. And how do we get back? By going to the beginning,
the first commandment: "I am the Lord, thy God. Thou
shalt not have false gods before me." Benedict and
Bernard were about the business of shattering false gods
and promoting the intense faithfulness Yahweh commands
of us. In beginning Chapter 4 of his Holy Rule, a section
called "The Instruments of Good Works," Benedict begins
a list of seventy-two items with: "First of all, to love the
Lord thy God with all thy heart, with all thy soul, and

with all thy strength."

But what of this thing called stability?

To most of us, the connotation of this word means something like "to stay in one place." Well, that's a big part—a very central part—of the Benedictine/Bernardine way. Even if the modern monk is out on assignment for a weekend or for a year or more, he has a home to return to—an unchanging base that helps one stay firm or stable in an ever-changing world. This, in fact, is a most important facet of the stability definition: There is a stability not only to a place but also to the unchanging commitment to the people who live there. Our growth as individuals depends in no small way on our relationships and the stability of those relationships. In the larger sense, still, there is the Great Relationship, the Ultimate Relationship, and our stable commitment to that. Being rooted in the love of God is the ultimate stability.

The love that binds us to God and roots us in stability is described by Bernard in timeless prose:

> Love is sufficient for itself; it gives pleasure to itself, and for its own sake. It is its own merit and own reward. Love needs no cause beyond itself, nor does it demand fruits; it is its own purpose. I love because I love; I love that I may love. Love is a great reality, and if it returns to its beginnings and goes back to its origin, seeking its source again, it will always draw afresh from it, and therefore flow freely.[4]

It seems that especially in our modern culture, we who are out in the world struggle with this issue of stability all the time: Do I come or do I go? Should I or shouldn't I? We live in a world of options, a world of changes—perhaps far too many options and changes! When all one has to do to completely change one's mind is to hit the delete button on a computer keyboard, how can we learn to make wise choices and how can we help our children make wise choices?

I propose we keep our perspective by putting the question into the context of this Benedictine virtue of stability. By that I mean allowing ourselves to dream, of course, but also allowing that God just might want us to "leave our lives alone" and "bloom where we are planted." Benedict seemed to propose that all the good that we can do in life can pretty much be done in the place where we reside: "The workshop wherein we shall diligently execute all these tasks is the enclosure of the monastery and stability in the community."[5] Benedict was making a statement that, yes, the grass on the far-off hills may look green indeed, but don't neglect looking at the grass under your feet right now and digging in there.

Does this mean there is no room for movement or change or dreaming in one's spiritual lifetime? Far from it. Saint Benedict had a dream; Saint Bernard had a dream. You have a dream. But there is a time for wondering and wandering and a time for hunkering down. I have a writer-friend who works at this hunkering down in the spiritual life very hard. And it's especially hard for her because she is the consummate dreamer. And yet frequently when she is asked what she's been doing, her favorite answer is, "I'm practicing being content." Very Benedictine!

But also very Benedictine is the understanding that local interpretations, adaptations and applications of the Holy Rule are both very human and necessary. Ironically, part of what has made the Benedictine institution so stable is the fact that it is flexible and adaptable (sort of like the high-rise buildings in an earthquake zone: the ones that are strong yet flexible are the ones that stay standing!). So it is the nature of the Benedictine Rule that it yields to interpretations within each monastery or congregation.

Ultimately, then, the lesson for you and me is that we, too, can draw individual applications for our own lives. So for you the ultimate message of Benedict might be to join a small faith community and observe the Liturgy of the Hours on a regular basis; for your neighbor it might mean reciting Psalms 4 and 90 each night, joining monks and nuns and others throughout the world in their Compline prayer; for another it may mean becoming a Benedictine Oblate or associate, a lay follower and embracer of Benedictine values; for me and my wife and children it may mean having a sacred prayer space or heart room in our home.

Let it be a place to sustain you, to help you persevere, to give this thing called fidelity or stability a fighting chance.

Kathleen Norris, in her wonderful book, *The Cloister Walk*, concludes a late chapter by telling readers about her encounter with a very old and ill Benedictine monk in a monastery infirmary. Just before she enters his room, a nurse announces to the monk that he has a visitor. Norris overhears the monk say, "Ah...it's a sweet life." And then he repeats it as she enters the room. Norris tells it so beautifully:

> The elderly monk in that hospital bed would probably be startled to hear how beautiful he was to me as he lay there with a hideously bruised face; how he radiated the love of Christ.... I don't know what he was like as a young man, but I'm sure he struggled, like every other Benedictine I've known, to become a monastic person. He'd probably hasten to assure me that he struggles still, that he is still in need of spiritual guidance and correction in pursuing "conversion of heart," a vow unique to the Benedictines.[6]

For Reflection

- *What is your unique "monastery," the "enclosure," for you at this time in your life? Do you find yourself burrowing in there and mining it for all its riches? Or is it more like a burrowing in and a spinning of wheels?*

- *Thanks perhaps to Cecil B. DeMille and his* The Ten Commandments, *all I could think of for years and years as a false god was that golden calf that the Hebrews built. God and the Old Testament writer were speaking figuratively, of course. But there are false gods we create in our lives everyday. Who are, what are your false gods?*

- *Is it any wonder that in today's mobile society, where all of us are being relocated and moved many times, we crave community and stability? Would you list stability as one of the things you believe in or crave? If not, what do you crave?*

On Being Renewed

How you have been inflamed anew by the fire of God, how from weakness you have risen to strength, how you have blossomed afresh into a holy newness of life! This is the hidden work of the finger of God, sweetly renewing and wholesomely changing the spirit within you, not indeed from evil to good, but from good to better.[7]

Closing Prayer

Gracious God,
our prayer today is that we
remain faithful,
that's all.

Help us seek you and your will alone.
Help us recognize the
false gods that society puts up
in front of us, that we ourselves
worship from time to time.
May you, Lord,
only you,
be glorified in all things.
Amen.

Notes

[1] Thomas Moore, *Meditations: On the Monk Who Dwells in Daily Life* (New York: HarperCollins, 1995), p. 38.

[2] John McQuiston, *Always We Begin Again* (Harrisburg, Pa.: Morehouse Publishing, 1996), p. x.

[3] *Saint Benedict of Nursia: A Way of Wisdom for Today* (Paris: Editions du Signe, 1994), p. 1.

[4] Harvey Egan, S.J., *An Anthology of Christian Mysticism* (Collegeville, Minn.: The Liturgical Press, 1991), pp. 176-177.

[5] *The Holy Rule of St. Benedict*, Chapter 4.

[6] Kathleen Norris, *The Cloister Walk* (New York: Riverhead Books, 1996), p. 366.

[7] Saint Bernard of Clairvaux, Letter to Richard of Fountains, trans. Bruno Scott James, *The Letters of St. Bernard of Clairvaux* 241, no. 171, as cited in William O. Paulsell, "Bernard of Clairvaux as a Spiritual Director," *Cistercian Studies Quarterly* 23 (1988): 229.

Going Forth to Live the Theme

> Lord, now let your servant go in peace;
> your word has been fulfilled:
> My own eyes have seen the salvation
> which you have prepared in the sight of every people:
> A light to reveal you to the nations
> And the glory of your people Israel. (Luke 2:29-32)

Thus do the Benedictine and Cistercian monks I have come to know over the years conclude their day. With this verse at Compline (Night Prayer) the monks go quietly into the night to rest in peace, joy and in their declared faith in God's sure love.

And thus do we conclude our reflections and prayer using Saint Benedict and Saint Bernard as our guides. Both Benedict and Bernard have shown us that our journey through life can be not only a path *to* God but *with* God. They show us that the way is not easy, but it's clearly lighted; the path is not wide, but it's clearly passable; the way is not short or smooth or perfectly climate-controlled. And yet, each step of it is clearly holy—if we ask God to make it so by walking it *with us*.

Ora. Labora. Silence. Simplicity. Solitude. Humility. Obedience. Conversion. Community. Faithfulness. These are some of the stepping stones on our path. And the list goes on. Let us say with Benedict and Bernard: If these be the stepping stones to *seeking God alone—together*, then, my friends: *Procedamus!* Let us proceed!

Deepening Your Acquaintance

To learn more about monastic life, about Benedict and Bernard and Western monasticism and its influence:

Kelty, Matthew, O.C.S.O. *My Song Is of Mercy*. Kansas City, Mo.: Sheed and Ward, 1995.

_____. *Sermons in a Monastery*. Kalamazoo, Mich.: Cistercian Publications, 1983.

Lawrence, C. H. *Medieval Monasticism: Forms of Religious Life in Western Europe in the Middle Ages*. Essex, England: Longman, 1989.

Merton, Thomas. *Entering the Silence: The Journals of Thomas Merton, 1941-1952*, ed. Jonathan Montaldo. San Francisco: HarperSanFrancisco, 1996.

Norris, Kathleen. *The Cloister Walk*. New York: Riverhead Books, 1996.

Pennington, M. Basil, O.C.S.O. *Monastery: Prayer, Work and Community*. San Francisco: Harper & Row, Publishers, 1983.

To learn more about Benedict, specifically, consider these resources:

Chittister, Joan D., O.S.B. *The Rule of Benedict: Insights for the Ages*. New York: Crossroad, 1993.

De Waal, Esther. *Living With Contradiction: Reflections on the Rule of St. Benedict.* New York: Harper & Row, Publishers, 1989.

_____. *A Life-Giving Way: A Commentary on the Rule of St. Benedict.* Collegeville, Minn.: The Liturgical Press, 1995.

Howard, Katherine. *Praying With Benedict,* Companions for the Journey Series. Winona, Minn.: Saint Mary's Press, 1996.

McQuiston, John. *Always We Begin Again: The Benedictine Way of Living.* Harrisburg, Pa.: Morehouse Publishing, 1996.

Vest, Norvene. *No Moment Too Small: Rhythms of Silence, Prayer and Holy Reading.* Kalamazoo, Mich.: Cistercian Publications, 1994.

To learn more about Bernard of Clairvaux, specifically, consider these resources:

McGuire, Brian P. *The Difficult Saint: Bernard of Clairvaux and His Tradition.* Kalamazoo, Mich.: Cistercian Publications, 1991.

Merton, Thomas. *Thomas Merton on St. Bernard.* Kalamazoo, Mich.: Cistercian Publications, 1980.

Further studies of Bernard and the Cistercian order to which he belonged are best obtained through Cistercian Publications, WMU Station, Kalamazoo, MI 49008.